P9-BAU-222

# DATE DUE

| | | | |
|---|---|---|---|
| | | | |
| | | | |
| | | | |
| | | | |
| | | | |
| | | | |
| | | | |
| | | | |
| | | | |
| | | | |
| | | | |
| | | | |
| | | | |
| | | | |
| | | | |
| | | | |
| | | | |
| | | | |

FOLLETT

# MAO'S
# LAST
# DANCER

# MAO'S LAST DANCER

# LI CUNXIN

YOUNG READERS' EDITION

Walker & Company
New York

Quotations on pages 61 and 72 are from the songs "I Love Beijing Tiananmen" and
"We Love Chairman Mao" (author's own translation)

"A Short Note on the Long History of China" written by Barbara Ker Wilson

First published in Australia in 2003 by Penguin Books Australia,
a division of Pearson Australia Group Pty. Ltd.
Published in the United States of America in 2008 by Walker Publishing Company, Inc.


For information about permission to reproduce selections from this book, write to
Permissions, Walker & Company, 175 Fifth Avenue, New York, New York 10010

Library of Congress Cataloging-in-Publication Data
Li, Cunxin.
Mao's last dancer / Li Cunxin.
p.    cm.
"First published in Australia in 2003 by Penguin Books Australia."
ISBN-13: 978-0-8027-9779-7 • ISBN-10: 0-8027-9779-2 (hardcover)
1. Li, Cunxin, 1961– 2. Ballet dancers—China—Biography. 3. Defectors—China—Biography.
GV1785.L475A3 2008        792.802'8092—dc22        [B]  2008006104

Visit Walker & Company's Web site at www.walkeryoungreaders.com

Book design by Cathy Larsen
Typeset by Post Pre-press Group
Printed in the U.S.A. by Quad/Graphics Fairfield
4  6  8  10  9  7  5  3

*To the two special women*
*in my life—my mother and my wife*

献给我一生中最亲爱
以及对我影响最大的两位女人：
我的母亲方瑞庆
和我的妻子玛丽。

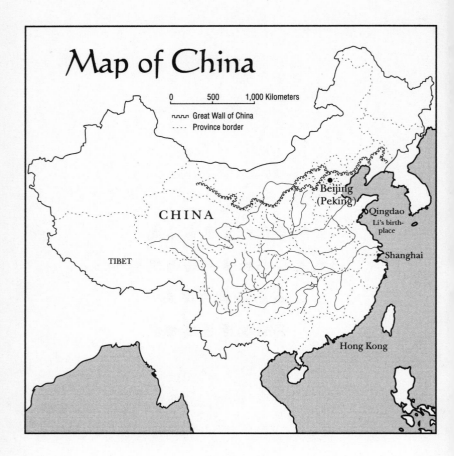

# Map of China

0   500   1,000 Kilometers

ᴧᴧᴧᴧ Great Wall of China
---- Province border

CHINA

TIBET

Beijing
(Peking)

Qingdao

Li's birth-
place

Shanghai

Hong Kong

# CONTENTS

# PART TWO
## Beijing

# PART THREE
## The West

# A WEDDING

## QINGDAO, 1946

On the day of her marriage, eighteen-year-old Reiqing sits alone in her village home. The wedding has been arranged by marriage introducers, as is the custom. Today the bride will meet her groom for the first time. She worries that her future husband will not be kindhearted and will not like her. But most of all she worries about her unbound feet. Bound feet are still in fashion. Little girls as young as five or six have to tuck four toes under the big toe and bandage them to stop the growth. The tighter the feet are bound the smaller they will become. The girls are so crippled they have to walk mostly on their heels. When Reiqing's mother tried to bind her feet, she defied her and ran away. But what will her future husband and in-laws think about her unbound feet?

The groom is twenty-one. He leaves home before sunrise. Strong men are hired to carry two sedan chairs from his village to the bride's. There are trumpets, cymbals, gongs, and bamboo flutes.

The bride is almost in a panic by the time her groom arrives. He wears a dark blue cotton gown and a tall hat. Silk flowers are pinned over his heart. He kneels, and kowtows three times, bowing his head all the way down to the floor, facing north, in the direction of the god of happiness.

A feast follows. The cost of the meal will break the bride's family's finances. Many relatives and friends chip in, but the favors and debts will have to be repaid in years to come.

While the groom's people feast, the bride sits on her bed, her *kang*, away from everyone. A silk veil conceals her face. This is called the "quiet sitting." She wears a long dark maroon gown, with pink silk flowers sewn onto it. She has no jewelry; her family is too poor.

Toward the end of the meal, the bride's mother brings her a bowl of rice, a double-sided mirror, and ten pairs of red chopsticks. The bride has to eat three mouthfuls of rice, and spit the last mouthful into her mother's pocket. She has to keep some rice in her mouth to last all the way to her in-laws' house before she can swallow, symbolizing that she will never starve along the entire journey of her life. Then she puts eight pairs of chopsticks into her mother's pocket. The remaining two pairs she keeps, the

ones with chestnuts and dates tied on them. These symbolize the early arrival of sons.

The bride cannot stop shaking. Tears stream from her
eyes. Soon she will become a wife and another family's
daughter-in-law.

"You silly girl," her mother says to her. "Don't cry!
You're going to a family with enough food. Do you want
to be poor for the rest of your life?" She gently wipes her
daughter's tears and hugs her. "I'll always miss you and
love you. Take good care of your husband and he'll take
good care of you. Obey him and make him happy. Bear
many sons. Be kind to your mother-in-law." She lowers
the veil over her daughter's face, and leaves, feeling nothing but pain.

The bride sobs quietly for the first half of her journey to
the groom's village. She has never left home before. At the
halfway point one of the carriers shouts, "Flip your mirror!"
She takes the mirror she's been given and flips it over: now
she should forget her past and look forward to the future.

When she arrives at the groom's gate, a metal bowl on
the table in the center of the courtyard is flaming with fire.
The groom gets out of his sedan chair and waits for his bride,
her face still concealed by her veil as she is helped out of her
chair by two of his sisters. They walk together toward the
table while a local wise man reads aloud an ancient poem.
Few people understand it because few of them have ever
gone to school. The bride and groom kneel on two bamboo

mats and kowtow. The groom then takes his bride's hands and helps her up. She cannot see the flames from the bowl on the table, but she can feel the intense heat, symbolizing the fire of passion, the fire of love.

Before the bride takes her first step with her husband, the groom's fourth brother gently brushes the soles of her shoes with an iron filled with burning coals, to give her warmth from the end of her body right up to her heart. Led by her husband, she walks slowly toward the door, where there is a horse's saddle. They have to cross over it together. The bride cannot see through her veil and is afraid she will trip. The saddle symbolizes hard times in life, which they will overcome together. Her husband squeezes her hand. "Stop. Now lift your foot," he whispers. She pulls up her gown to her knees and steps over safely. But her heart sinks. She has shown her unbound feet to the entire world! Her in-laws will be disgusted.

Her husband feels her hesitation. "Let's go to the kang," he says gently.

On one of the corners of the kang sits a triangular wooden box. Inside are different kinds of grains: wheat, corn, rice, millet, sorghum . . . they represent the hope that the newly-weds will have plenty of food throughout their lives.

All day the bride has longed to remove her veil. Now she is afraid. Her husband may not like her appearance. Nervously she lifts her veil. For the first time in their lives they look at each other. The bride sees that her husband is handsome. There is something honest and humble about him too; he immediately captures her heart.

The groom, Li Tingfan, is stunned by his bride's beauty. They sit there until their "widen your heart" noodles arrive, which symbolize acceptance of each other's fortunes and faults. Then comes the "warming your heart" rice wine and they drink from each other's cup with crossed arms.

The groom's brothers, their wives, and his sisters come forward one by one to wish the newlyweds a happy life. The groom's youngest sister, who is about the same age as Reiqing, whispers, "I'm so happy to see your big feet! I've got them too!" She winks at her new sister-in-law and flies out of the room, giggling. Reiqing is overjoyed.

The groom is called away to the wedding banquet, while the bride begins her "sitting through the time." For three days she sits, legs crossed in a lotus position, back straight, for every waking hour. Many relatives, friends, and neighbors visit during those three days.

On the fourth day, the bride takes her new husband to visit her own family. They like their new son-in-law, and are happy for their daughter. "Don't look back," her mother tells her. "Now you belong to the Li family."

When Reiqing gets into the back of the cart and looks back at her familiar village for the last time, she has no tears. Her name and place are changed forever. Her destiny lies ahead.

So it was for this bride and groom, my mother and father, in Qingdao in 1946. My mother looked at her strong husband in the front of the cart and felt lucky and proud. She leaned over to him to ask if she could sit beside him. Without a single word, he moved over to the side and let his new bride sit close.

# PART ONE

## My Childhood

# Home

My parents, as newlyweds, lived in the New Village, near Qingdao, in Shandong Province. The Li family, together with all the other villagers, had been forced to move here by the Japanese invaders during World War II. The Japanese built an airport where my father's family used to live. Now, a year after the end of that war, the village was controlled by one of the peasant communes that had been set up by China's central communist government.

My parents lived with my father's six brothers, their wives, his two sisters, and their children—over twenty people crammed into a six-room house. As the youngest daughter-in-law, my mother's status in the Li family was the lowest. She worked hard to prove her worth.

Often she would not see my father until late in the evenings, because he worked at two jobs, either away in the fields or carting building materials, all day long. The family would sit for dinner by candlelight, the men eating at one table and women and children eating at others.

The women of the house would sew, wash, clean, and cook. The speed and quality of my mother's work won her mother-in-law's approval. To cook well was a sign of love and care. My mother was often sent to deliver the food to the men in the fields, because of her unbound feet. Her sisters-in-law envied her such freedom.

My mother's mother died within the first year of my parents' marriage, so my mother would visit her father once a year, even though he never loved her in the same way as he loved his sons. A son could work in the fields, bring home a daughter-in-law, and carry on the family line.

My parents continued to share a house with my father's family. Their first son was born about a year after their marriage, their second just over two years later, their third two years after that, and their fourth in 1955. My mother eventually came to be known as "that lucky woman with seven sons."

My family's crowded house had a small front courtyard. Inside were four rooms: two small bedrooms, a slightly larger bedroom, and the kitchen/living room with two built-in woks. There was no refrigeration and no running water, only a huge clay pot for storing drinking water. The woks backed onto the bedroom walls, which were covered with newspaper and contained the chimneys. Fire and smoke would travel through the walls on the other side to retain heat, but as the night wore on our beds became colder.

The floor was reddish earth. During wet weather, water always seeped in and my father would have to dig out the wet floor and wait for a dry day to replace it with new earth, pounding it down with a huge wooden hammer.

Clothes were stored in papier-mâché boxes my mother made, stacked on the two small beds during the day and moved onto the floor at night. There was also a main kang, about the size of a small double bed. Eventually my parents and all their sons had to share those three beds. The main bedroom was also the room where my family ate.

After waking each morning on the freezing beds, we would fold the blankets into rolls and tuck them neatly away. What remained was a bamboo mat. A wooden tray would be placed on the mat and the family would sit around it, crosslegged, to eat each meal.

My family went to one of the village wells to fetch water, carrying it in two buckets that hung from either end of a bamboo pole balanced across one shoulder. The adults and the big boys would carry big buckets, the little boys smaller buckets. Water was heated in the big wok, and basins were used for baths. (There was a public bath in the commune shared by over ten thousand people, but my family couldn't afford to use it.) We had no bathroom, only a toilet—a hole in the ground in the front courtyard.

You had to stand or crouch on two wooden boards, one on each side of the hole. There was no roof, so it was freezing cold in winter. Half the toilet was inside the wall and half outside, to allow the waste to be collected and taken to the fields as fertilizer. The village crap-man poured the waste into his wheelbarrow, which he pushed through the narrow streets. People would move aside to allow him to pass. One day he had a collision with a bicycle. The foul contents of the wheelbarrow ran all over the street. What a stink! Even after the neighbors washed the area over and over, everyone avoided that street for a long time. Neighbors tried to have him replaced, but nobody wanted to be the next crap-man.

My family had to make use of every inch of their front yard. There was a small vegetable patch, climbing beans on the stone walls, and a pigsty with a couple of very thin pigs. There was never enough food to feed the people, let alone the pigs. There was also a chicken yard, but the chickens never had enough food to produce many eggs.

The commune allocated each family in the village a piece of land. My family's was one twentieth of an acre, halfway up the Northern Hill, about fifteen minutes from home. It was so small it could only be used to grow essential foods such as corn and yams. On Sundays, our entire family worked on this land with my father. Everything was done by hand using shovels, picks, hoes, sickles, and ploughs.

The villagers had no say in what to plant: the central

government in Beijing decided that. My family's area planted mainly wheat in the winter; corn, yams, and sorghum the rest of the year. The government would get the biggest portion, at a set price. The rest was divided among the peasants according to the number of members in each family and how many points the family earned during the year. The most a man could earn in a single day was ten points—about one *yuan* (equal to approximately seventeen US cents at that time). Women received about half a man's earnings.

One year, there was a severe drought and nobody was paid a single yuan. The village had to borrow money from the local government to lend to every family so they could buy food to survive. It took more than two years to repay that loan, and still the peasants had to eat anything that moved, and some things that didn't, including tree bark.

My family was very poor, but there were even poorer people in our commune. By the time I was born, three years of Mao's Great Leap Forward and bad weather had resulted in one of the greatest famines the world had ever seen. Nearly thirty million Chinese died. My parents were desperately fighting for survival.

⁂

I was my parents' sixth son, born on January 26, 1961. By then my parents had been married for fifteen years. Our na-na, my father's mother, lived next door, and his fourth brother (we called him Fourth Uncle) lived next to her. Our third uncle's family lived in front of us. He died quite young, leaving four young girls and a boy. My father, who we called *Dia*, and our fourth uncle became their de facto fathers.

When I was just fifteen days old, my mother, who we called *Niang*, left me on our kang, wrapped in a cotton quilt, before going to the kitchen to make her bread rolls for the Chinese New Year. Mothers in China always wrapped their babies' arms tightly against their bodies and laid them facing up. That day my niang had so many rolls to steam that the kang where I was lying became boiling hot. I struggled my right arm loose, and the kang badly burned the middle of my arm.

When my niang first heard my screams, she thought I wanted milk. She had none left in her breasts so at first she did not respond. By the time she came to check on me, the elbow area of my arm was severely burned and blistered.

Two days later, my arm had swollen up and turned bright red. My parents could not afford to take me to the hospital. I developed a high fever and screamed day and night. Finally they had to borrow some money from our relatives and friends to take me to the hospital. "Your son has a bad infection," the doctor informed my parents. "Your only hope is to apply some herbal medicine."

"What will happen if it doesn't work?" my niang asked, desperately afraid.

"He may lose his right arm," he replied.

My parents purchased herbs from a local medicine shop. My niang followed the doctor's instructions and stewed them in the wok. They applied the dark liquid to my arm. It made the infection worse.

My niang started to panic. She took me to see many healers who lived in our area, to no avail. Then my fourth aunt said, "An old healer told my mother once that *bai fang* helps infections." Bai fang was a meat tenderizer, full of acid. My desperate niang decided to give it a try.

When she applied the bai fang I screamed like a stuck pig. She couldn't bear to see her son suffering such pain and stopped the treatment.

But my fourth aunt still believed it would work. "*Ni tai sin yuen la!*" You are too soft-hearted, she told my niang. She locked her door, crushed the bai fang into a powder, and rubbed massive amounts onto my raw, exposed muscles. I screamed nonstop. Every hour she would wash my arm with warm water and reapply bai fang.

Years later my niang confessed, "I was outside your fourth aunt's door and my heart bled each time you screamed. The sound of your cries was like a thousand sharp knives cutting into my guilty heart! Several times I banged on your fourth aunt's door, trying to take you away. Thank the gods for her determination. She just ignored me."

My fourth aunt nearly gave up many times that day. But her determination saved my arm. A large scar remained, and in years to come, in moments of crisis, I would touch it. It became my link to my niang, a reminder of her love.

Three years later, my niang gave birth to her seventh son, my youngest brother, Cungui, whom we called by his nickname, "Jing Tring." My parents knew they couldn't provide enough food to feed the sons they already had. Every family was allocated a very small quantity of meat, seafood, and eggs, along with oil, soy sauce, sugar, salt, wheat and corn flour, rice, and coal each month. Often they were not available at all.

We ate a lot of dried yams. They were the easiest things to grow. I was often woken up at five o'clock in the morning to go to the yam fields with my big brothers before they started school for the day. We each carried a shovel and a bamboo basket. We dug for any yams that might have been overlooked by the peasants during harvesting. The hope of those yams for breakfast kept us going. Often the fields had already been turned over by others in equally desperate circumstances, and we returned home with empty baskets.

During summer, every family's front yard and roof was covered with slices of these yams drying in the sun. Some people even laid them out on the street. But if rain came, they had to pick them all up quickly: if they got wet, they soon turned moldy. Once dried, the sliced yams were stored in a huge clay pot.

We had dried yams, steamed or boiled, almost daily, week after week, month after month, year after year. They had no taste and stuck in our throats. Dried yams were the most hated food in my family—but there were others in the commune who could not afford even dried yams. We were luckier than most. Luckier than the thirty million who starved to death. Dried yams saved our lives.

We rarely ate meat. Once a month we would wait in long lines at the market for the fattest piece of pork available.

Mealtimes in my family were always sad for my niang. There was often nothing for her to cook. Out of respect for our elders, we would always wait for our dia to start. One day, when my niang served dinner, it was clear there was not enough food for everyone.

"I don't feel hungry," our dia said. "I had a good lunch."

Each of us had our chopsticks in hand, but we hesitated. Our niang gave our dia an annoyed look and made "*zhi, zhi, zhi*" sounds with her tongue. "Don't you dare not eat! Your health is our entire family's security. We will all only drink water if you starve yourself to death!"

"I'm not hungry," our dia protested.

Our niang picked up some food with her chopsticks and put it in our dia's bowl. We started to eat only after he took the first bite. Our parents always ate slowly to allow us more food. On many occasions our niang told us to leave the best food for our dia because he was our bread-winner. But our dia told us we should give the best food to our niang: if it were not for her we would all have only "north-west wind" for dinner.

It was always like this. Seven pairs of hungry eyes would

look at our parents, but we all knew how difficult it was to get any food at all.

To survive, my niang worked every spare hour she had in the fields, as well as cooking and looking after her boys. Often she had to swallow her pride and borrow food from relatives or neighbors. She could make delicious dishes from anything . . . except dried yams. I loved watching my niang cook. I could talk to her alone then, and have a little bit of undivided attention. I would ask her many questions about the cooking, and learned when to add certain spices and how to cook well.

Despite our poverty, our parents always taught us to have dignity, honesty, and pride. Our good family name was sacred and should be protected with all our might.

One day when I was about five, I went to play at a friend's house. Sien Yu was the same age as me. His uncle, who lived in the city, had brought him a little toy car, and Sien Yu let me play with it for a while. I loved it so much. When he went inside to get a drink, I took it and ran home.

"Where did you get that?" my niang asked suspiciously.

"I . . . I found it on the street."

She knew I was not telling the truth. No one in our area could afford to spend money on a toy. She took my hands firmly and pulled me back to Sien Yu's house. She said to his mother, "Is this your son's toy car?"

Sien Yu's mother nodded.

"I'm sorry, I think my son has stolen it," my niang said.

"Don't get upset," Sien Yu's mother replied. "Your son is too young to understand."

"I'm ashamed of what my son did!" said my niang, and apologized profusely. She tried to make me do the same, but I felt too embarrassed. I tried to escape from my niang's firm grip. I wanted to run away. I hated my niang for embarrassing me like this. She shouted. She wanted the entire world to know I had stolen my friend's toy car. I screamed and kicked as she dragged me home.

As soon as we went inside our house, she pulled me to her chest, hugged me tightly in her arms, and sobbed. It was as though she had suffered as much humiliation as I had. "I'm so sorry to do this to you," she whispered tenderly. "I'm so sorry we are too poor to buy you a toy car." After a brief moment she continued: "I'm too stupid to have all of you in this cruel world! You don't deserve this suffering!" I felt her tears streaming onto my hair.

I hated to see her so sad. "I'll have enough food for you one day! I swear it!" I vowed to myself.

That evening, at dinner, my dia started lecturing us. "Although we have no money, no food, and can't buy clothes, and although we live in a poor house, one thing we do have is *pride*. Pride is the most precious thing in our lives. Throughout our forefather's struggles, the Li family always had a good reputation. I want every one of you to remember this: never lose your pride and dignity no matter how hard life is."

# My Niang and Dia

Memories of my niang and my dia are always related to how hard they worked. Our dia was often up before five-thirty in the morning, and my niang had to be up even earlier to cook him breakfast. With all the cooking, washing, and sewing she had to do, she hardly had time or energy to pay each of us much attention. We fought over her love and affection. Besides cooking every meal, she made all our clothes and our quilts and blankets too. She carried the laundry either to the stream about twenty minutes south of our house or to a dam up on the Northern Hill. Our patched clothes were always clean. She took immense pride in making her seven sons look well cared for.

Every aspect of life was hard for my parents. There was a great shortage of black coal throughout China. The small amount allocated to us barely lasted through the winter, making the inside of our house colder than the frigid outdoors. We also had to sleep in the same bed. Jing Tring and I slept with them until I was eleven. All four of us, head-to-toe. I hated my brother's smelly feet right by my face and he must have hated mine more since I was taller than he was. Yet I loved sleeping with my parents. It felt so safe.

Because of this hard life, I rarely saw a smile from my niang, but when I did, my heart would blossom like a lotus flower.

My niang was recognized as one of the best seamstresses in the village. My parents simply had no money to buy ready-made clothes, and my niang didn't have a sewing machine. The older ladies would teach the younger ones, and they often gathered together as a sewing group in our house to drink tea and gossip. My niang's sewing skill was admired by many. Her stitches looked as if they *were* made by a sewing machine—small and perfect.

My niang was an open-minded person, receptive to new ideas. Mao's Cultural Revolution boasted that one of the great achievements of the Red Guards had been the establishment of evening schools aimed at teaching the uneducated peasants Mao's communist ideas. We were all given copies of *The Quotes of Chairman Mao*, which everybody called the Little Red Book. I was six years old then and I remember two enthusiastic young Red Guards coming to teach my niang to read. She never learned to recognize words, but she could memorize entire paragraphs of Chairman Mao's sayings. She would practice while she was washing, cleaning, sewing, and cooking: I often saw her lips moving as she silently recited passages. She was considered a model student.

One day, while my niang was trying to make a fire to cook dinner, two young Red Guard girls came into our house to check on her progress. She was having a terrible day and couldn't get the half-burned coal to light. She was polite and explained that she didn't have time just then and asked them to come back another time. Just as she was going to start cooking, the two girls came back to test my niang on her understanding of the Little Red Book. They had to report back to their group leader.

I could see my niang's anger growing. Eventually, she handed one girl her wok flipper and asked her to take over the cooking. The two girls just stood there and looked very confused. By now my niang was at the end of her patience. She roared at them: "I could learn Chairman Mao's sayings every day, all day long, until I die, but who is going to do my cleaning, washing, and cooking? Who will bathe my sons, sew their clothes, cook for my family every day of the year? Do you think Chairman Mao's words will fill our stomachs? If you can come back every day to help me do all of *these* things, I will learn whatever you want me to!"

The two girls left, red-faced. That night my niang told my dia what she'd said to the two girls. He just smiled. The girls never returned to our house again.

By the time I was eight, hard work and poverty had begun to wear down my niang, strong as she was. She woke one morning complaining of dizziness and didn't eat any breakfast. My youngest brother, Jing Tring, and I were home with her. She had planned to do a lot of washing that day, so she packed up a heavy clay basin full of clothes and with a washing-board under her other arm, headed off to the dam on the steep Northern Hill.

I begged her not to go. "I'll fetch you some water so you can do your washing at home."

"It will be slippery at the well with all the ice around it. Do you want to die in the well?" she replied impatiently. She walked out the door.

A couple of my friends came over to our house to play that morning. Then, around noon, a neighbor rushed to our house, shouting, "Hurry! Your niang has fainted half-way between the dam and your house!"

My dia was not yet home from work; often he had to finish his quota of lifting heavy materials for the morning before he was allowed to take his lunch hour. That morning he'd said he would try to get back for lunch because he knew our niang wasn't well.

I asked my friends to look after Jing Tring, then rushed to my fourth uncle's house, but the door was locked. In a panic I rushed to another neighbor's house, but realized immediately she would not be able to help: she had tiny

17

bound feet. It would take her all day to walk up the rough dirt road. Then I ran as fast as I could toward the dam. Tears streamed down my face. I was afraid I was too small to be of any help.

I found my niang lying on the side of the road, her clay basin broken, the pile of washed clothes scattered around in the dirt. I shook her violently. "Niang! Niang, wake up!" I shouted, panicking, fearing she was dead.

A few minutes later she slowly opened her eyes and asked me, in a weak whisper, "Where is your dia?"

"He is not home yet!" I replied, frightened, but relieved she was alive.

She sighed. "Help me up."

I was too small to be of much help. I held one of her hands to support her but after a few wobbling steps she crashed to the ground again. I felt useless.

"I'm going to have a little rest here," she said. "Go home and see if your dia or any of your brothers are back."

I flew home. No one was there. I rushed around trying to find help. Eventually I saw a man riding his bike home. "Da . . .Ye! Are you in a hurry?" I stuttered.

"Not particularly. Why?" he replied, puzzled.

"My niang fainted on the Northern Hill and can't get home. Please help her. She is dying! Please! I beg you!"

"Don't worry, leave it to me." He hopped onto his bike and pedaled off as fast as he could, with me running behind. He reached my niang and was already on the way down with her, propped on the back of his bike. I quickly gathered up all the clothes but had nothing to carry them with. I wrapped all the long pieces around my neck, waist, and arms, and carried the small pieces against my chest on the wooden washing-board. Those muddy clothes were extremely heavy but I managed to get everything home.

By the time I arrived, my fourth aunt and some other women had already begun to put cold wet towels over my niang's forehead.

That was the first time I ever saw my niang ill. She couldn't get out of bed for nearly a week. The "barefoot doctor" in our village gave her medicine she had to take three times a day with warm water. The barefoot doctor was one of Mao's inventions, a product of the Cultural Revolution. They were supposed to live among the peasants, live *like* peasants. Their precious shoes wouldn't be useful in the muddy fields, and that is why they were known as barefoot doctors. By the early 1970s, facing a severe shortage of doctors and nurses in the countryside, Mao ordered clinics and hospitals to train as many people as possible and send them to the countryside. He criticized the medical profession for avoiding the communes.

Despite the barefoot doctor's medicine, my niang's fever wouldn't break, and she kept having dizzy spells. I often placed my hands onto the frosted window and then onto my niang's burning forehead to help cool her down.

That week, my dia had to cook, wash, clean, and get my

brothers ready for school. Dinner was always late since he had to finish his day's quota before he could come home. My dia's cooking was very basic but nobody complained. We knew how serious my niang's illness was. I was so frightened my niang might die. "Look after your dia if I don't make it," she said. "Maybe I will die young, like my mother."

Everyone in the family, all the way down to five-year-old Jing Tring, was expected to pull his weight. My niang was worried that my dia might get sick from overworking: we would not survive if he got sick. But he never showed any signs of fatigue though he was very quiet.

Over the next few weeks, my niang gradually recovered. Exhaustion and starvation were the likely causes of her illness. Her health was never quite the same; she suffered from dizzy spells ever after. My dia wanted her to stop working in the fields, but the reality was that our family couldn't live on my dia's wage alone. Eventually he agreed to my niang working in the fields part-time, to ensure our survival.

Every day except Sunday, my dia would ride his old bike to work in the town of Laoshan. It was a good half-hour away. He had paid someone in the flea market ten yuan for that beloved second-hand bike. It was so precious to him that we were never allowed to touch it. He had to carry all kinds of heavy materials—huge grain sacks, big pieces of stone—as part of his job. He was also the driver's right-hand man: when the truck had to reverse he would guide the driver, sitting alongside. I was very proud of him. A truck was impressive—most transport was still done by horse and cart in the communes. His job was considered one of the better-paid jobs in the county and many people were envious of him. He was paid thirty-five yuan per month, almost $4.20 then! I wished that I could be a truck driver one day, but I knew at the bottom of my heart that my destiny lay in the fields as a laborer.

It was often well after seven in the evening before our dia came home. He would be worn out, and my niang often had to massage him at night to prepare him for the next day. He never missed a single day's work.

My parents didn't go to school when they were children, so they could not read to us. But nighttime was still story time, and our dia would tell us stories and fables. We always listened eagerly.

My brothers also played their own version of I Spy. One of them would select a word from the newspapers glued all over the walls, and whoever spotted this word first would have a turn to select the next. Sometimes we wouldn't find the word for days. We always thought it sad that our parents didn't join in because they couldn't read.

My dia was always patient and emotionally controlled, sometimes stubborn, but always good-tempered. The only time I remember him losing his temper with us was when my fourth brother's teacher came to report to our parents about his bad school marks that year. Cunsang knew his teacher's report wouldn't be good. He gathered together my fifth brother, Cunfar, my youngest brother, Jing Tring, and me and said, "Let's make chaos! I hate her, and she doesn't like me either!" We needed little encouragement. The teacher sat on one end of the kang and my niang on the other. Our dia poured them a cup of tea each. As soon as the teacher started to tell my parents of my brother's poor school progress, we began running from side to side on the kang and screaming.

Our dia gave us a dark look. "Be quiet," he said.

"I'm sorry about our misbehaving children," our niang apologized.

After a few quiet seconds, Cunsang whispered in our ears: "She let out a loud fart the other day and pretended it wasn't her!" We laughed uncontrollably. "Farter, farter, smelly farter!" we shrieked.

The teacher pretended she didn't hear, but our parents were terribly embarrassed. "You will be in trouble if you make any more noise!" our niang threatened us.

"All boys are wild," the teacher said. "I don't know how you cope with so many of them."

A few minutes later I knocked the teacher's cup over and spilled tea onto her clothes. We were like three wild animals.

Eventually the teacher had had enough. "I have to go now. I have other families to visit tonight," she said, giving us a disgusted look. My parents continued apologizing to her on her way out.

As soon as she was gone, my niang turned to my dia. "Lock the door!" she screeched. "Kill these wicked boys! I can't believe how bad they are!"

Jing Tring started to cry, so she removed him from the kang. "The little one is too young to understand. It's not his fault. Just kill the big ones! See if they dare do it again!"

My dia stormed into the room with a broomstick in his hand and closed the door. I had never seen him so angry. His face was frightening enough, let alone the flailing broomstick. He hit us with that broomstick so hard that I wanted to dig a hole in the ground and hide.

My niang kept urging him on from the other side of the door and we kept screaming. "We won't dare do it again! We won't dare do it again! We promise!"

Our niang's head popped in and out of the room like a yo-yo. "Teach them a lesson! See if they will ever dare to do it again!" We didn't know then that she thought we looked so comical she was laughing her head off outside, but she had to pretend she was angry with us. What a lesson that was: we never misbehaved like that again.

# THREE

# A Commune Childhood

By 1969, the poverty around Laoshan had worsened. I remember going with my friends to the beach one day, an hour's journey on foot, to find clams and oysters or, if we were lucky, a dead fish. We each carried a bamboo basket and a small spade.

Many people were already there, also searching. After about half an hour we'd found nothing except empty sea-shells. The beach was clean and bare.

Halfway home I suggested to my friends that we should make a detour and sneak into the nearby airport to try and find some half-burned coal. This was the airport the Japanese had built during the Second World War. Now there were only a few People's Liberation Army guards there. The Japanese had used coal and half-burned coal as part of the filler under the runway, and the outer part had already been dug away by desperate people. Since then the guards had tightened security.

There was a line of big trees along the edge of the airport and a small ditch. The ditch was dry at that time of year and we crept along it for about fifteen minutes, bending down so the guards couldn't see us.

Digging for half-burned coal was like digging for gold. Eventually our baskets were full. But carrying heavy baskets with a bent body proved too difficult for us eight-year-olds. About halfway out, one of the boys slowly straightened up and was spotted by the military guards. They immediately fired bullets into the air and started to chase us. We dumped our baskets and spades and ran for our lives.

Our winters in those days were bitterly cold. As well as having to cope with the lack of coal, we also had to deal with lice. They lived with us in our cotton quilts, coats, and pants. Unlike our summer clothes, which our niang washed regularly, our quilted winter coats and pants couldn't be washed because they were made with cotton-wool pieces that would have shriveled up in the water.

The only real way to combat lice was to keep clean. Every weekend our niang would heat up huge woks of water for us and tip it into a wooden washing basin. Each of us had a piece of washcloth, and we'd soap our bodies and help to wash each other's backs. If one family member had lice, the rest of the family would too: they multiplied so quickly. Everyone in China scratched constantly. In the evenings after we took off our clothes and got under the

quilts, our niang always flipped our clothes inside out, trying to kill the lice with her thumbnails. But she could never
get rid of the lice completely.

I don't ever remember going to a doctor or hospital
during my childhood; not that I didn't get sick, but we
could never afford it. The only time I got close to a medical
person was waiting for a barefoot nurse to give us small-
pox shots. We had to wait in long lines in our commune
square with our sleeves rolled up. The nurse used the same
needle to inject everybody, and small pieces of alcohol-
soaked cottonwool to clean the needle heads and our skin.
Crying wasn't an option, no matter how much it hurt.
When I cut myself I was told by my parents to swipe my
fingers on the windowsill to gather some dust to put on
the cut and stop the bleeding. This was our Band-Aid and
antiseptic all in one.

Our niang's remedy for severe coughs involved eating
a shed snakeskin wrapped around a piece of green onion.
The snakeskin was like tasteless plastic and looked disgust-
ing. It always made me want to vomit, but it was the most
effective treatment for sore throats and coughs we had.

Despite our hardships, there were also joys in our chil-
hood. The one time we all looked forward to, the one time
when we would be guaranteed wonderful food, was the
Chinese New Year.

Our niang had to make and steam many bread rolls

26

for the Chinese New Year, as gifts for our relatives. She made them in the shape of fishes and peaches, representing peace and prosperity, and gold bars, representing wealth. The bread rolls would split if the dough had not been kneaded perfectly. She would be too embarrassed to take the split ones to our relatives, so we kept those for ourselves.

Before dark on New Year's Eve, my dia and my fourth uncle would take me and my brothers to my ancestors' graveyard. We took bottles of water, representing food and wine, and stacks of yellowish rice paper stamped with the shape of old gold coins. We carried paper lanterns. Our pockets were filled with firecrackers. We spread the rice papers and stuck incense on top of each grave. After we lit the incense, we would kneel in front of each tomb and kowtow three times, calling out each ancestor's name, following a strict order, starting with the eldest and ending with the youngest.

"Dia, how can the dead people hear us if they are dead?" I asked.

"They know," he replied with his usual brevity.

Just before we went home for our special dinner, we asked each of our ancestors to follow us there for the New Year's holiday. Our dia and our fourth uncle poured out the bottles of water in front of each grave. On the way back we made sure our lanterns were brightly lit, so our ancestors' spirits could see clearly the road ahead. We lit the firecrackers to wake up the ancestors. "*Xing gan wo men hui ia. Lu bu ping. Man man zou.*" Our dia and our uncle would ask our ancestors to walk slowly and not trip on the uneven road. They talked to our ancestors as though they were still alive. My brothers and I thought this was funny but we had to take this occasion very seriously. Our ancestors' spirits lived on because they had been kind people before they died. They had the power to help us and influence our fate.

The meal that night was Niang's favorite to cook, because this was the only time she had enough good ingredients. Cold dishes came first: marinated jellyfish with soy sauce and sesame oil; seaweed jelly with smashed up garlic and soy sauce; salty peanuts and pig-trotter jelly. Then hot dishes: fried whole flounder, and a delicious egg dish with green chives and rice noodles. There would have been at least ten eggs in it! It just melted in my mouth. There were vegetable dishes too, and they all had small pieces of meat in them. The aroma of all this delicious food, mixed with the Chinese rice wine, the incense and the pipe smoke, was unforgettable. And it only occurred once a year, on that special Chinese New Year's Eve.

Everything was special and magical. Everyone chatted enthusiastically, but the one who talked the most that night was our dia. Happiness filled everyone's hearts. We would forget hardship. We felt privileged. There were always too many dishes to fit on the wooden tray. How much could we eat in one night?

The meal always ended with steaming pork-and-cabbage dumplings. They looked precious and smelled exquisite! I always saved plenty of room for them. They truly were a labor of love. Our niang would put a one fen coin into one dumpling and whoever found it was destined to have luck throughout the year. One year nobody found that fen, even though our niang swore she'd put it in. Did someone eat it without even noticing? We swallowed those dumplings as if we were wolves.

The very first bowl of dumplings was lucky food, for the gods of the kitchen, of harvest, prosperity, long life, and happiness. The second bowl of dumplings was for our ancestors. Before our niang placed each of these bowls at the center of the table, with incense on either side, she would pour some broth onto the ground in four directions. "Gods, our kind gods," she would murmur, "please eat our humble food. We are blessed by your generosity." The square table was always placed in the middle of the room. Before Chairman Mao and the Cultural Revolution, we would have displayed a family tree and a picture of the god of fortune on the northern wall above the table. But this tradition was now considered a threat to communist beliefs. Any family doing this would be regarded as counterrevolutionary, for which there were heavy penalties, including jail.

Nobody was to touch those dumplings my niang left at the center of the table . . . yet they always mysteriously disappeared overnight. "The gods and our ancestors have eaten them," our niang would say.

After the meal we would go from house to house to pay our respects and wish everyone a happy and prosperous New Year. Every gate in the village was wide open. Nobody was supposed to sleep. We would play tricks on our friends if we caught any of them sleeping. After midnight, firecrackers could be heard everywhere. Thousands of small red and white pieces of firecracker paper splattered the streets.

On New Year's Day we would sleep until midmorning. Everyone was exhausted, but the holiday spirit lived on.

The second day of the New Year we would light lanterns and incense and show our ancestors the way back to their graves.

The fifteenth day of the New Year was always dreaded. It marked the beginning of our harsh life once again. From ancient times this night was traditionally the "Night of Lights." We would walk around the house and shine torches into every corner to keep away evil spirits.

Since the weather was very cold and the fields frozen after the holiday, there wasn't much work to do on our little piece of land. Our main outdoor activity during these days was kite flying. I often sat myself apart from the other kite-flying boys. For them this was just another game, but for me this time was special. My kite was my secret communication channel to the gods.

Our dia was an expert kitemaker. He made very simply shaped kites: a square, a six-pointed star, and a butterfly. I adored making kites with our dia. He would take us up to the Northern Hill and tell stories from his childhood. One of our favorites was "The Frog in the Well."

There was a frog that lived in a small, deep well. His well and the sky he could see above it were his entire universe.

One day he met a frog who lived in the world above. "Why don't you come down and play with me. It's fun down here," the frog in the deep well said.

"What's down there?" the frog above asked.

"Everything. You name it. The streams, the undercurrent, the stars, the moon." The frog on the land sighed. "My friend, you live in a confined world. You haven't seen what's out here in the bigger world."

The frog below was very annoyed and went to ask his father if this were true. "Please don't tell me there is a bigger world out there than ours!"

"My son, the world up there is enormous. But our destiny is down here. There is no way we can get out."

The little frog was determined. "I can get out! I can!" He jumped and hopped, but the land above was too far away.

The poor little frog spent his whole life trying to escape

31

from the dark, cold well. The big world above remained only a dream.

I thought about that poor frog in the well many times. Like him, we had no way out. I felt sad and frustrated.

So I would use my kite to send messages to the gods. I found refuge from the freezing wind in a ditch and took out my pocketful of small paper strips. I wet both ends of the paper with my tongue and looped each strip around the string of the kite. The strong wind pushed my paper loop up toward the kite.

The wish I sent up with my first paper loop was for my niang's happiness. I told the gods that she was the kindest, most hardworking niang, but she was so poor. I challenged the gods: if they really existed, then they should change my niang's situation. I would get angry with the gods for not being fair to my niang. Then I would become frightened, and beg them for forgiveness. After that, I would send a second wish, for my dia's good health.

My last wish was my most important of all. I looped a third piece of paper around the kite string, and wished to get out of the deep, dark well. I daydreamed about all the beautiful things in life that were not mine. I begged them for more food for my family. I begged the gods to get me out of the well so I could help my family. My imagination traveled far beyond the faraway kite in the sky.

My messages to the gods often got stuck at the knots in the string along the way. I had to jerk the string to get them past the knots. Often I was the last one to leave the freezing fields on the Northern Hill. But it was my imagination that kept my heart warm and my hopes alive.

# Seven Brothers

My brothers and I were like all other boys, fighting at times and getting on each other's nerves. But the bond between us was strong: we were expected to love and care for each other, to be happy for each other's achievements. The older brothers were expected to look after the younger ones and the younger ones to respect the older.

Our dia and his fourth brother had grown up very close too, although my dia was nearly eight years younger. My fourth uncle and aunt could not have children; out of love and compassion my parents agreed to let them adopt their third son. So, before he was two years old, my third brother, Cunmao, was given to my uncle and auntie, a couple of houses away. We always thought we were cousins.

When Cunmao was a teenager, he found out the truth.

I was feeding our hens that day when Cunmao stormed into our house. "Where is my seventh niang?" he shouted—that was what he called my mother.

"She is sewing on the kang," I told him. He looked so strange that I quietly followed him.

"Why did you give me away? Why not one of the others?" I overheard Cunmao demand angrily.

"This was decided even before you were born," our niang replied gently. "You were not singled out. I love you just like my other sons."

"I want to come back!" he said.

There was silence. "You cannot," our niang said at last, her voice quivering.

"You're my niang. I want to come back!" he said.

Our niang let out a long sigh. "I beg you to forget that I'm your real mother! Do you think it is easy for me to see you around every day? Go back and love your parents. They love you. You're luckier than your brothers. At least you have enough food to eat."

"I'd rather be starving with you than living apart from you!" Cunmao said.

"Your parents would be destroyed if I took you back now! I shall always love you as one of my sons whether you're with us or not. But you must first love them and bear a son's responsibilities toward them. You may then love us too if you desire."

Silence again. After a moment she said, "Come here." And through the window I saw them hug each other.

I ran away then, and hid in a cornfield. I couldn't believe my third cousin was really one of my own brothers. My eyes filled with tears, and from that moment on I regarded Cunmao as one of my real brothers.

In the end Cunmao respected my parents' position and remained a faithful son to my uncle and aunt.

My eldest brother, Cuncia, we called Big Brother. He was thirteen years older than me. I was only four when, in August 1965, he was sent to Tibet by Chairman Mao.

In the 1950s there was a popular uprising in Lhasa, which was suppressed by the Chinese military. Now, a decade later, Mao was sending hundreds of thousands of his young Red Guards there.

In his absence, my second brother, Cunyuan, took on the responsibilities of the eldest son. Cunyuan, however, wanted to be free. He too wanted to go to Tibet, but my parents would not allow it. They needed his earnings and were desperate for a daughter-in-law to help our niang with the domestic duties. So they arranged his marriage to a girl from our first auntie's village. Our aunt told our parents that this girl was hardworking and would be a perfect match for Cunyuan.

But Cunyuan was in love with another girl. Her father was a district official. When she found out about the arranged marriage, she immediately came to our house. "Uncle, Aunt," she said respectfully to my parents, "I have known Cunyuan for four years. I love him and he loves me! I beg you not to force him to marry someone he doesn't love."

"Young girl, you are too young to understand what love is," my niang replied. "My son is not worthy of you. There is no future working in the commune."

"Aunt, I *do* know what love is! I will follow Cunyuan to the end of the earth. I'm willing to eat grass as long as I can be with him. Please give us a chance!"

"You come from a different background," my dia told her. "You would not like our poor commune life."

"I promise you I will be a faithful wife and a good daughter-in-law!"

But my parents felt strongly that this girl came from a family that was too good for us.

Cunyuan resented the way our parents had arranged his marriage and his relationship with them suffered terribly.

My fourth brother, Cunsang, wasn't the cleverest among us. Our niang blamed an accident he'd had as a baby, when a stack of chairs crashed down on his head, for his poor school results. I loved my fourth brother: he was kind, honest, and loving, and he was the only older brother who didn't mind me sitting beside him while he played card games.

It was my fifth brother, Cunfar, who was the closest to me. We were two and a half years apart—and we fought over everything. But I loved him. He was my protector against bullies, my partner in games, and my rival in races.

So I grew up with my brothers, playing outside, under the sun, in the rain, even in the freezing winter. Summer was my favorite time. Except in winter, I hardly ever wore shoes for the first nine years of my life.

One day, late in the afternoon, the sun was setting and we were playing hide-and-seek in the village. I was climbing on people's walls and roofs, trying to find a good place to hide. I climbed over our six-foot-high stone wall, trying to get behind the three-foot clay pots where the pigs' food was stored. One of the pots stored fermented millet waste. My foot slipped on the loose stones of the wall, I lost my balance and fell headfirst into the pot of thick, gooey waste. I was only about seven or eight, not much taller than the pot.

Our niang was busy cooking dinner and my fourth brother was her helper. By chance, Cunsang looked out and noticed the shadow of a pair of feet struggling upside down on the toilet wall. He immediately rushed to the pot and pulled me out. "You could have found a better place to die than the millet pot!" he said.

I was gasping for air, seconds away from losing my life.

The streets, the riverbank, the dam, and the hilly fields were our playgrounds. We made our own spinning tops and loved playing marbles. Of course, we often had to help our dia, working our small piece of land. Sometimes we worked on it in the rain, trying to capture as much rainwater as possible in buckets and pots. In winter, when the fields were covered with thick, thick snow, we built snow-men and had snowball fights, chasing each other wildly around. We would roam for hours in this white world, in the vast open space of the fields, with snow falling around us, and return home covered with snow, our ears, noses, hands, and feet bright red from the cold and our bodies steaming with sweat under our quilted cotton clothes. More washing and mending for our niang.

One Sunday, in the middle of a summer drought, my brothers and I had just finished helping our dia carry buck-ets of water to the yam crops. We were sweating and the hot sun burned our skin, so our dia allowed us to go to the dam to cool down. As the fastest runner I got there first. Some of the older village boys were already splashing in the middle of the dam. The water level was low. The other boys were treading water, but it looked as though they were standing. Without thinking, I dived in. I had never learned to swim, and I panicked when I couldn't touch the bottom. Every time I tried to yell for help, I would swallow some water, my head going up and down. One of my cousins was with the group of older boys. He saw me struggling and quickly swam to me and pulled me out of the water. A minute later I would have drowned.

About the middle of 1966, Mao's Cultural Revolution reached its most chaotic period. Jing Tring and I were too young to participate but my three eldest brothers did.

They would go out in the evenings and return late at night. They told me horror stories about the young Red Guards, how they burned and destroyed anything that had a Western flavor—books, paintings, artwork—and tore down ancient temples and shrines. Mao wanted communism to be our only faith. The young Guards had only to mention Chairman Mao's name and they would not have to pay for a thing. For a brief period, they nearly bankrupted China and the country teetered on the edge of civil war. Back in the New Village, however, we knew little of that wider picture.

My parents tried their hardest to persuade my brothers to stay home on those evenings. But in reality there was nothing they could do—an unstoppable political heatwave was sweeping through China.

Then, one day, the well-respected head of our village was accused of being a counterrevolutionary. My brothers and I watched as a group of other counterrevolutionaries were paraded through our village, with blackboards around their necks and tall, pointed white paper hats on their heads. Their crimes were written in chalk on the blackboards and their names were written on their hats. They had to stand on a temporary platform in the center of the commune square and confess their crimes to the huge crowd. We went along to watch. The officials and Red Guards handed out propaganda papers. One man kept shouting propaganda slogans with a handheld speaker. People were shrieking and jeering. During their confessions the accused had to lower their heads to avoid the objects thrown at them. If anyone looked up, he would be regarded as arrogant or too deeply influenced by capitalist "filth." They could do nothing right: if they spoke softly, they were smacked and accused of hiding something; if they spoke loudly, they were kicked and accused of having an "evil landlord-like attitude."

Their confessions were often disrupted by the man with the handheld speaker, who shouted revolutionary slogans such as "Knock down and kill the capitalists!" or "Never allow Chiang Kaishek and the landlords to return!" "Never forget the cruel life of the old China! Always remember the sweet life of the new China!" And of course there were the endless "Long live Chairman Mao!" slogans. The revolutionaries constantly pulled the counterrevolutionaries' heads back up to humiliate them even more.

My parents told us that the head of our village was a good man. I couldn't understand what crime he could have committed. But a few days later, the communist revolutionary leader led a big crowd to the head villager's house. I joined the crowd. Only then did I realize that he'd been missing from the group of accused during the parade and rally.

The door of his house was locked and the leader banged on it, screaming, "Open the door, open the door!"

Eventually the door opened. His wife stood there,

begging for mercy. She told the communist leader that her husband was so sick he couldn't even get out of bed. The leader didn't believe her. He demanded to see him. When he did he became convinced that the head villager was indeed very sick. A few years later, I remember seeing him sitting by his gate on a little chair. He looked pale and motionless. He'd lost all his hair. I felt desperately sorry for him, but by that time I too had become one of Mao's young Guards, and I felt guilty for even thinking that way.

I witnessed many rallies and parades during the Cultural Revolution. The Red Guards said they were killing the class enemies, which included the landlords, factory owners, successful businessmen, Guomindang Party members and army officers, and intellectuals—anyone who might pose a threat to the communist government. There was one particular rally that still, to this day, makes my heart bleed. My friends and I heard the communist leader read out the sentences for about fifteen landlords, factory owners, and counterrevolutionaries. Then they were loaded onto a truck. We could see their pointed white hats, with their names written on them in black ink and a big red cross struck through each name. They were taken to a nearby field. Despite the adults' warnings, my friends and I followed as fast as we could.

I saw the men standing against a mud wall. Someone started counting. Two of the men crumpled onto their knees. One started to scream, "I'm innocent, I'm innocent!

Let me live!" Another screamed, "I have young children! They'll starve to death without me! Have mercy for my family!" Then I heard someone shouting, "*Yi, er, san!*" One, two, three . . . Guns fired. The sound ripped through my heart. I saw blood splatter everywhere. The bodies fell down. I screamed, and ran home as fast as I could.

I wished I had listened to the adults. I wished I'd never witnessed this. It haunted me in many of my dreams.

# FIVE

# Na-na

Chairman Mao's regime not only changed the way we lived; it also changed the way we died.

One day when I was still about eight, I wanted to impress my niang by cooking lunch for the family when she was late coming back from working in the fields. So I placed some of the leftover food on a bamboo steamer. To see if the food was properly cooked, I lifted the big, heavy wok cover. I was so short that I had to stand on a little stool. As I lifted the cover, the stool fell from under my feet. Steam from the wok gushed into my face. I crashed forward and my niang's six precious newly purchased plates were knocked to the floor, smashed.

I was terrified! I knew it had taken my parents all year to save enough money to buy those plates. And now, there they were, in a thousand pieces on the floor. Was I ever in trouble! I ran to Na-na's house next door. If we were ever in trouble, we'd go to Na-na's.

"What's wrong?" she asked.

"I've broken Niang's new plates!" I sobbed.

"How many did you break?"

"Six."

"*Oh! Wo de tian na!* My god!" she exclaimed. "How did you manage to break all six?"

I quickly told her what had happened.

"Don't worry. I'll take care of it." Na-na looked at me reassuringly. "You broke those plates trying to help your niang. You're a *good* boy. You shouldn't be punished for this." Then she murmured to herself: "What a world we're living in now. A mother of seven has to work in the fields! I've never heard of such a thing!"

I went out to play, and when I returned home that afternoon my niang was very upset. I heard her sigh to my dia, "Our niang was trying to help cook our lunch. She accidentally slipped off the stool and broke all our new plates!"

"Is she all right?" Dia asked, concerned.

"Miraculously, she didn't hurt herself at all."

I was eternally thankful to my na-na for saving my skin. I quietly slipped into her house that evening and whispered in her ear, "Thank you, Na-na!"

"*What?*" she shouted.

I was so afraid others might find out the truth if I said it any louder, so I just gave her a big kiss on her bony cheek and went back home.

My na-na's health became progressively worse for the next half year. She couldn't walk, she became unable to eat, and she gradually slipped away from us. She died about a year after I broke the plates.

As was the local custom, her body was laid in a coffin in her living room, for three days. The smell of incense filled our houses.

"Why does Na-na's body have to stay here for three days?" I asked my third brother, Cunmao.

"In case she comes alive again."

"How can a dead person come back to life?"

He told me a story then, which he'd heard from a friend: "An old couple were looked after in their old age by their only son and daughter-in-law," he began. "They were not well cared for. Most of the time they were given leftovers to eat. Not all people are as kind to their elderly family members as we are. One day, a distant relative of the old couple took pity on them and quietly slipped two hard-boiled eggs into their hands. They were so excited that they quickly peeled the shells off and just as they were going to eat them they heard their daughter-in-law coming toward their room. The wife told her husband to hurry up and eat his egg. Fearing their daughter-in-law would accuse them of stealing the eggs, the old man quickly put his in his mouth and swallowed it whole."

46

"Why didn't he chew it?" I asked Cunmao.

"He didn't have any teeth left. The old man choked on the egg and instantly stopped breathing."

"Was he dead?" I gasped.

"Of course he was dead!" Cunmao replied. "So they bought him a cheap coffin and had a cheap burial."

I could tell the best part of the story was still to come.

"The old lady's only treasure was a pearl necklace her husband had given her and she wrapped it around his neck. The old man's son didn't wait for the three-day period. He buried his father the first night after his death. The word spread wide about the buried treasure around the old man's neck. At midnight, a robber dug up the grave and opened the coffin. He could see the pearls reflected in the moonlight. Before he took the necklace the robber made sure the old man was truly dead by punching hard on the old man's chest three times. Just as he reached for the necklace . . . Guess what happened?"

"The old man's son showed up?"

"Ha-ha!" Cunmao laughed heartily and shook his head. "The old man suddenly opened his eyes wide and said in a loud voice, 'What do you think you're doing, young man?' The robber, as if he had seen a ghost, jumped out of the grave and bolted away."

I sat there petrified. This was the last outcome I'd expected. Cunmao opened his eyes wide, just like the old man.

"Why did he become alive again?" I asked, terrified.

"I knew you wouldn't get it!" Cunmao scoffed. "The egg got stuck in the old man's throat and when the robber punched him, it was knocked loose so he got his breath back. And that's why we have to leave Na-na's body here for three days, in case *she* comes alive again too."

"Then why didn't anyone punch our na-na three times?"

"Do you think our elders would do it in front of us? Okay, go and play now."

When I asked my second brother Cunyuan about the reason for our na-na's three-day staying, he told me it was so relatives who lived far away could see her before she was buried. I thought Cunmao's story was more satisfying.

I was stricken with grief at Na-na's death. She had told my parents, a few days before her death, 'If there is one thing I want you to do for me when I'm dead, it is to bury me properly.' She firmly believed that her spirit would live on in a different world. So my dia and uncles asked a good carpenter to make a special coffin, carved with birds, flowers, trees, and water. Our youngest aunt's husband, who is a furniture painter, painted it.

It wasn't easy to obtain permission for Na-na's burial since this was now considered an old, unhealthy tradition. The government had started forcing people to cremate the dead. Na-na's burial was the last one allowed in our village.

The village leaders let us select the edge of a ditch for her burial site. It was a water escape channel. Any place with water was a lucky place.

Before she died, Na-na had made her own funeral clothes, shoes, and other essential burial items. Na-na's daughters dressed her in her dark greenish blue cotton jacket and black shoes with flowers stitched on the soles. The man with the best handwriting in the village wrote Na-na's name on a large piece of white paper, the same shape as the stone nameplate on the grave. Once a person died, his or her spirit would linger, looking for the place where they belonged. If we didn't have her nameplate put up quickly, her soul might wander away and become lost forever. At least one person would stay by the coffin at all times during those three days, to "keep the beloved company." Any person related to Na-na had to cry loudly as soon as they walked into the room. The person who was "keeping the beloved company" had to cry as well, and as they cried they would call out the visitor's name so Na-na would know who was paying her their respects.

As soon as the sun went down on the first day after her death, the entire family formed a procession. Everyone cried loudly all the way to a miniature temple, about ten minutes away from our house. The Red Guards had destroyed all the real temples, so my dia and uncles had to make this one. Here the local god would determine if our na-na was worthy of a happy life. If there were a god, he would definitely look after my na-na. She was the best na-na in the world. I couldn't imagine anyone kinder.

This procession was repeated again on the second night after sunset, and very early on the third day, when skilled diggers went to the burial site before sunrise.

The funeral itself was expensive. Our family hired coffin carriers; dancers on stilts; musicians; blanket-and-quilt carriers; even people to carry mirrors, combs, cups, food, drinks, and a lot of fake paper money.

The procession began from Na-na's house. Only men were permitted to go to the burial site. The women were left to cry in the house and cook the feast. My eldest uncle carried a big clay pot on his head. At one point he had to drop the pot on the ground. It broke in pieces, the signal for everyone to begin crying, one of the occasions when crying in public was acceptable.

The Li funeral entourage was impressive. Many distant relatives appeared, some we didn't even know existed. The procession moved slowly behind the coffin, all the way to the gravesite. I had never heard or seen my dia cry before. We had to kneel in front of Na-na's coffin and kowtow three times before she was lowered into her grave.

We had to wear something white for a whole year after Na-na's death. Our parents wore white shirts, but for us children the only things our niang could afford were white strips of cloth sewn onto our shoes. We often went to visit

Na-na's graveyard so she wouldn't be lonely in her new world. Each time, we brought her lots of symbolic money and food. I loved going back to her grave to wish her a happy life, but it always saddened me too.

Within a month of Na-na's death my niang suddenly fell ill. Despite seeing a few local healers, her sickness persisted and on the second night she had a strange dream: Na-na accused her and my dia of not looking after her. She complained that her house was shabby and the roof leaked. My niang tried to reason with her. "We looked after you to our best ability while you were alive and gave you a lot of money for your new world. What else can we do?"

"Who told you I'm dead?" my na-na snapped.

The next morning my niang told one of her sewing friends about her strange dream. "Maybe she needs help," her friend whispered in her ear. "Why don't you do a test to see if I am right?"

After her friend left, my niang took out a pair of chopsticks and an egg and placed the chopsticks pointing north on her kang. She lit two sticks of incense, closed her eyes, and called out: "Niang, mother of Li Tingfang, if it was you who showed your spirit last night, please show your spirit again now." Then she placed the egg between the chopsticks with the pointed end down. The superstition held that if it was Na-na's spirit calling for help, the egg should continue to stand up on the pointed end all by itself.

My niang opened her eyes and was stunned. The egg was still standing up!

For a few moments she didn't know what to do, until the egg fell and started to roll toward her. She grabbed it in her hand, as though it were Na-na's spirit, and immediately kowtowed three times in the direction of Na-na's burial place. "Niang! We will come to see you soon and bring you food and money! Please forgive us!" she murmured.

When my second brother arrived home from school that day she asked him to take two of his younger brothers to check on Na-na's grave straightaway. Three of us raced each other to the burial site and found a large round hole there, dug by an animal. We were not aware of our niang's dream then, so we simply filled the hole and told Niang what we'd found. As soon as our dia came home from work, she said to him urgently, "Go to our niang's grave with some food and money, and make sure the hole is properly secured. I will explain later!"

My dia went back to the grave, carrying a shovel, a bottle of water, some incense, and paper money.

Later that night our niang finally told us her dream and her test with the egg. All of us children laughed and thought she was just being superstitious, but our dia was more thoughtful. "One cannot fully believe it and yet one shouldn't disbelieve it."

"That's what Confucius would have said," I thought. Our niang's fever receded the very next day.

My parents discussed this incident often. So did our niang's group of friends, whose superstitious beliefs gave them hope beyond the harsh reality of daily life.

The death of Na-na was the first time in my life that I lost someone I loved dearly. Every time I entered or passed her house, tears would stream down my face. I kept hearing her sweet voice. I dreamed about her often.

# Chairman Mao's Classroom

The year my na-na died was the year I was supposed to start school. The compulsory age was eight, but there was no room for my group that year, so I didn't start until a year later.

It was February 1970. I had just turned nine. For my first day at school, my niang dressed me up in my best clothes, a new black cotton quilted winter jacket, hand-me-down cotton pants with patches on the knees and the bottom, and a winter hat of cotton and synthetic fur. She also made me a schoolbag from dark blue cloth. My dia bought me two notebooks, one with pages full of squares for practicing Chinese characters, and another for math. He made me a wooden pencil box containing one pencil, a small knife, and a round rubber eraser. One of the most important requirements was the Little Red Book.

"This is a special day for the Li family!" my niang declared at breakfast. "The Li family has one more scholar today." She tilted her chin at me. "We're not sending you to school to play. I hope you'll learn more than your dia and your brothers did."

"Mmm," our dia said. "It wouldn't be too hard to do better than your dia."

"Listen to your teachers, be a good student. Don't lose face for the Li family. Make us proud," said my niang.

I felt apprehensive. School meant that I had to wear shoes and conform to rules. Deep down, like my dia and my brothers, I wondered what use an education would be to a peasant boy destined to work in the fields. How would school help my family's food shortages? I didn't need education to be a good peasant.

The school we were supposed to go to was about a mile from our village, but there wasn't a spare classroom there at first, so our village donated an abandoned, rundown house as a temporary classroom. The older boys told us it was haunted. I always wanted to peek through the window and see what was inside, but I chickened out each time.

Forty-five new kids from four villages were enrolled that year. When we arrived at our school, we all gathered outside. One teacher introduced the man beside her as our sports teacher and herself as our Chinese and math teacher. Her name was Song Ciayang.

"Students, this is a new beginning in your lives! I hope you will treasure this opportunity Chairman Mao gives you, study hard, and not let our great leader down."

We didn't learn anything that first session. We spent that entire first morning cleaning the floor and scrubbing the walls. Then, we were divided into several small groups and Teacher Song selected two captains. The girl captain was taller than nearly all of us in our area. The boy captain, Yang Ping, lived in the east part of our village. He was considered privileged because his grandfather had been in Mao's Red Army. My eldest brother had once been kicked by Yang Ping's father from behind during a fight. Yang Ping's grandmother had apologized profusely, but I was determined not to make friends with Yang Ping. Anyway, by the time we had selected our own spot and placed our stools next to whoever we wanted to sit with, our first day of school was over.

Next morning we started at eight o'clock. Teacher Song called out our names one by one from her roll-book and we all obediently answered "*Ze!* " Then she picked out the boys and mixed us in with the girls. I had chosen a spot at the back with two of my best friends. Now I was sandwiched between two girls I didn't even know.

Teacher Song handed out our textbooks. "Students, welcome to your first official lesson." She paused. "Do you know who this is?" She pointed to Mao's picture.

"Chairman Mao, Chairman Mao!" we all shouted.

"Yes, our beloved Chairman Mao. Before we start our first class each day, we will bow to Chairman Mao and wish him a long, long life, because we wouldn't be here if it wasn't for him. He is our savior, our sun, our moon. Without him we'd still be in a dark world of suffering. We will also wish his successor, our second most important leader, our Vice-Chairman Lin Biao, good health, forever good health. Now, let's all get up and bow to Chairman Mao with our hearts full of love and appreciation!"

We all stood up, took our hats off, bowed to Mao's picture, and shouted, "Long, long live Chairman Mao! Vice-Chairman Lin, good health, forever good health!"

"Before you sit down," Teacher Song continued, "we need to perform one more school rule: I'll say 'Good morning, students,' and you will say 'Good morning, Teacher.' Let's have a practice. Good morning, students!"

"Good morning, Teacher!" we replied in unison.

She smiled. "Good! Now sit down. Raise your hand if you have the Little Red Book."

Most of us raised our hands.

"Those who don't have one, please ask your parents to buy you one. I want all of you to have them tomorrow. This is very important. We should follow Vice-Chairman Lin's example and never go anywhere without Chairman Mao's Red Book. It will give us guidance in our lives. Without it we will be lost souls."

Teacher Song continued: "Now you will learn how to read and write. Raise your hand if you can do so already."

I looked around. Very few students raised their hands:

mostly girls. I was relieved. I, for one, couldn't recognize a single word in my textbook.

"Please open the first page of your textbook," Teacher Song instructed.

A big colored picture of Chairman Mao stared out at me, occupying half the page, with shooting stars surrounding his face, as though Mao's round head was the sun. The bottom half of the page had words on it.

"Can anyone read the words on this page?" the teacher asked. The same girls raised their hands again.

"What does the first line mean?" Teacher Song asked the girl sitting to my right.

"Long, long live Chairman Mao!" replied the girl in a proud voice.

"Good, very good!" Teacher Song paused. She glanced over the class. "Yes, we want to wish Chairman Mao a long, long life, because our great leader saved us. I'm sure your parents have told you many stories about the cruel life they lived under Chiang Kaishek's Guomindang regime. Those were cold, dark days indeed. That government only cared for the rich. Children like you couldn't even dream of sitting here, but Chairman Mao made it possible for everyone to have this privilege. Today, I'll teach you how to write 'Long, long live Chairman Mao, I love Chairman Mao, you love Chairman Mao, we all love Chairman Mao.' I'll now write this on the blackboard. Pay special attention to the sequence of the strokes." She turned to the blackboard and wrote several lines with furious speed.

I was stunned. I didn't understand the strokes at all! I turned to look at one of my friends. He drew a circle around his neck with his right hand and pulled upward, his eyes rolling and tongue hanging out, as though he were being hanged.

"Now I want you to repeat each phrase after me." Our teacher pointed to the first line of words with her yard-long stick. "Long, long live Chairman Mao," she read.

"Long, long live Chairman Mao!" we repeated.

"I love Chairman Mao!" she read.

"I love Chairman Mao!" we replied.

We repeated the phrases again and again until we had memorized them for life.

For the next hour, Teacher Song explained in detail how to write each stroke of the words and the sequence we had to use. I picked up my pencil and realized that I didn't even know how to hold it. I looked to my right and copied the girl next to me, but I pressed too hard and broke the tip.

"Here, you can use mine," the girl next to me said. "I have three."

*Three*? She must belong to an official's family!

"What's the matter?" Teacher Song suddenly appeared in front of us.

"He broke his pencil," my deskmate answered.

"Oh dear, and you haven't written a single stroke yet," she said.

My face swelled up like a red balloon. Reluctantly I took the girl's pencil. Under Teacher Song's gaze I carefully placed the tip on the paper. To my horror the strokes popped out of my uncontrollable pencil like popcorn, ugly and messy, in all directions. They looked nothing like what was written on the blackboard.

"Let me help you," Teacher Song said. She placed her hand over mine and we finished "Long, long live Chairman Mao" together.

"Good. Now repeat these words five more times and you'll be fine," she said, and went to help some others. I quickly looked at my friend behind me. He shook his head in disgust and made funny faces. At least he felt the same as me.

The rest of the day went by excruciatingly slowly, and we only had a ten-minute break between each hour. Teacher Song's sweet voice went in one ear and out the other. Instead, my thoughts were out on the streets and in the fields. I couldn't wait for each ten-minute break to arrive.

During the final hour of our lessons that day, as I tried to write, I heard a bird chirping outside. I was always fascinated by birds. I would watch them and daydream. I admired their gracefulness and envied their freedom. I wished for wings so I too could fly out of this harsh life. But then I also thought of the constant danger of being shot down by humans or eaten by animals. And if I became a bird, I would leave my family. This would surely break my niang's heart. Yet sometimes I thought I might be able to help them more as a bird, flying high in the air and spotting food for my family.

My thoughts were interrupted by Teacher Song's voice. "All right, that's enough for today. I want you to practice what you've learned at home. Tomorrow, I expect you to remember what we've done today. Do you understand?"

"Yes!" we replied.

"Good. Now I'm going to teach you a song. I'm sure you will have heard it before. It is called 'I Love Beijing Tiananmen.'"

We'd heard this song many times over our village's loudspeakers:

I love Beijing Tiananmen,
The sun rises above Tiananmen.
Our great leader Chairman Mao,
Lead and guide us forward.

The singing became my favorite part of our day.

On the way home we exchanged our feelings about that first day of school.

"So boring!" one of my friends said.

"It's horrible!" said another.

"I hate sitting next to girls."

"What about the bird?" I asked.

"What bird?"

"Didn't you hear it on the windowsill?"

"I was struggling so much trying to write 'Long, long live Chairman Mao,' why would I hear a bird?" another friend replied.

We stopped at a sandy bank by the little stream south of our village and were surprised to discover that Yang Ping's group of friends had beaten us there and were playing "horse fight." We soon joined in. One person would sit on another's shoulders and opposing groups would try hard to unseat their opponents. Yang Ping and I, physically similar, were the "anchor horses" at the bottom. That day we were the last two standing on each team. We fought one another tooth and nail until we dragged each other down in a draw, totally exhausted, muddy, and with our clothes torn. Yang Ping and I struck up a good friendship after that.

＊

We spent our first two weeks of school in that temporary classroom until a room became available at the proper school. This consisted of single-story brick and stone classrooms joined to each other just like commune housing.

At eight that morning, the head of the school welcomed us and we were led by Teacher Song to our official classroom, a square room with two rice-papered windows on the outside wall. There was slightly more natural light here than in the temporary classroom; the ceiling was high and the air fresh. Pictures of famous communists—Marx, Engels, Lenin, and Stalin—were glued on the back wall. Large pictures of Chairman Mao and Vice-Chairman Lin Biao smiled warmly at us from above the blackboard, which was already filled with the words we were to learn that day. Under the blackboard was a concrete platform, and we had desks and small benches to sit on.

My fourth and fifth brothers were also at the school. It was my fourth brother's sixth and final year before he moved to the middle school. My fifth brother was in his third year.

After the first two weeks of school, I still had no idea what I'd learned or why I should study. Listening to Teacher Song babbling on just made me sleepy, especially in afternoon classes, which went from two until six. The only thing that kept me awake was the thought of playing with my friends during those ten-minute breaks.

After our second class one day, we were told to go outside for our first fifteen-minute physical education class, with all the other 250 students. The sports teacher stood in front of everyone, loudspeaker in hand and shouted out the eight exercise routines, accompanied by recorded music: simple arm and leg stretching exercises, which took no more than five minutes.

I found my fourth brother, Cunsang, as soon as we'd

finished. "How's it going?" he asked.

"It's boring! I hate it!" I replied.

"Join the tribe. Why did you think I wanted you to make chaos when my teacher came to our house?" He was reminding me of the time we received the broomstick beating.

"How can you understand the writing? It all looks like grass to me," I said.

He burst into laughter. "That's what I thought the first few weeks. It will get better, I promise."

I didn't believe him. "What's the use of learning words anyway?" I asked.

"I don't know," he replied honestly.

I followed him to my fifth brother's classroom on the opposite side of the school yard and found Cunfar in the middle of a pile of bodies, wrestling each other onto the ground.

"How was your first lesson, scholar?" he teased breathlessly as he dusted off the dirt.

"All agony, no fun," I replied.

"The math is even more fun!" Cunsang gave a wicked smile.

"Can't be worse than Chinese," I said.

"Just wait!" he replied as the bell rang for the next class.

I had prepared myself for the worst in our math class, but to my surprise the numbers were more bearable than the grasslike Chinese writing. Even so, I still preferred to dream of running wild outside and playing games with my friends.　🍃

I wasn't the best student in my year, but my classmates did vote for me as one of the first Little Red Scarf Guards in our class. We wore a triangular red scarf around our necks, and for this honor we had to qualify in Mao's "Three Goods": good study, good work, and good health.

I didn't learn much academic stuff during my time at school, except the many propaganda phrases and songs, and many of those I didn't understand. I really only lived for the two weekly sports classes. I was good at the sporting stuff. We had rope-skipping and track-and-field, which was mainly running, and by the second half of our second year, Teacher Song had selected Yang Ping as the captain of our class and me as vice-captain.

During those school years of mine, the central government released Mao's newest propaganda campaigns one after another. Often our school organized rallies when we would march around the villages playing drums, cymbals, and other instruments, carrying gigantic pictures of Chairman Mao and waving red flags. Everyone carried the Little Red Book, and we marched with pride. I felt so happy to be one of Mao's Little Red Scarf Guards. Once I was chosen to lead the shouting of the political slogans. When we passed our village, I glanced around and saw my niang and my fourth aunt standing in the middle of the crowd. I shouted at the top of my voice: "Long, long live Chairman Mao!" Other leaders shouted at the same time. It was completely chaotic, but we all wanted our mothers to see and hear us.

"Niang, did you hear me?" I asked her when I came home that day.

"How could I hear you? It was like a zoo out there!" she replied.

In October 1971, some shocking news about Mao's chosen successor came through our village's loudspeakers. Vice-Chairman Lin Biao's plane had been shot down over Mongolia. Lin Biao had been trying to flee to the Soviet Union when his evil motives were discovered. There was speculation that the plane he was on contained many top-secret documents. The most nerve-racking speculation was that there were factions of the military loyal to Lin Biao who could be attempting a coup to topple Mao's government.

We were told how close Lin Biao was to Chairman Mao. He had written the foreword in the Little Red Book, which he was said to have always had in his hand.

When we returned to our school that afternoon, all scheduled classes were suspended. We were summoned to the school yard. With microphone in hand, the headmaster read out a document from the central government. Lin Biao had been planning a major coup for a number of years and Chairman Mao had narrowly escaped several assassination attempts. How fortunate it was that our great leader was safe and that we would still be able to enjoy our sun, our rain, and our daily oxygen! We must study harder to strengthen our resolve so that we, the next generation of communist young guards, could carry the red flag forward.

After this speech, he ordered us back to our classes to study the Little Red Book for the rest of the afternoon. I, like all my classmates, was truly scared that if Lin Biao had succeeded, we would all live in the dark ages once more. This made me more determined to be a good young guard of Chairman Mao's. At dinner that night, we talked excitedly about Lin Biao's demise. But our parents' reactions were different.

"Who cares about Lin Biao!" our niang said. "All I'm concerned about is food on the table."

"Your niang is right," our dia chipped in. "Who has time to worry about the government? What we need is enough food to survive."

During my second year at school, we learned how to write "We love Chairman Mao" and "Kill, crush Liu Shaoqi, Deng Xiaoping, and the class enemies." I wondered how useful all this talk about Liu Shaoqi, the Chinese president, and his right-hand man, Deng Xiaoping, was meant to be.

Sometimes we'd write these things in chalk on the walls of people's houses. Over time, with people scribbling over each other's writing, all the words became muddled. Some of the older boys often wrote rude remarks about people they didn't like, and common family names such as Zhang, Li, Wang, and Zhou often got mixed up in the scribbling.

One day, an education official from the Qingdao government passed through our village and noticed some of the writing: "Kill, crush, Mao, Zhou, and Lai," it read. The official charged into the village office and demanded a thorough investigation. Many people were questioned by the police.

The next day, in the middle of our math class, our headmaster and two policemen came in and asked all the students who lived in the New Village to stand up. We didn't know what was happening. The headmaster told us to follow him to his office, where we were divided into two groups. The police questioned us for a whole morning about the writing on our village wall. I'd thought it was going to be about something much more important! Did you write on the wall? Did you see anyone else write on that wall? Have you seen any strangers in your village lately? Do you know anyone who may dislike Chairman Mao or Premier Zhou? I was puzzled. I couldn't imagine anyone not loving our great leaders.

The officials eventually let the matter go. But the police

appeared in our village quite frequently after that, and none of us dared write anything on the walls ever again.

It wasn't long after this, on the way home from school, that I found something that was to become my secret treasure. A book. Only about forty pages, lying on the street near the garbage dump. I picked it up and started to read the first page and couldn't stop. It was a foreign story translated into Chinese. I couldn't understand all the words but I could make out that the story was about a rich steel baron, in some place called Chicago, who fell in love with a young girl. I'd just got to the bit where he used his money to build a new theater when the pages ran out. How I wished I had the rest of the book! It was such delicious reading! Love stories were hard to find. The Red Guards destroyed any books that contained even a hint of romance or Western flavor. You would be jailed if such books were found in your house.

I locked those forty pages in my personal drawer, never realizing the danger I'd put my family in. I read them many times. I wondered how the people in the story could have such freedom. It sounded too good to be true. Even after hearing years of fearful propaganda about America and the West, the book was enough to plant a seed of curiosity in my heart.

To satisfy our need for stories, some friends and I turned to the opera and ballet storybooks that our older siblings were given at school. We would act out different characters, and especially loved the scenes with guns, swords, and fighting. Acting out the dying scene was always a delight! Everyone wanted the hero's role. We play-acted like this even before we started school in the mornings.

More spark for our hungry imaginations came from the touring movies. Once or, if we were lucky, twice a year, a small group of people from the Qingdao Propaganda Bureau would come to our village to entertain us with a movie about things like Mao's Red Army triumphing against the Japanese army, Chiang Kaishek's Guomindang regime, the struggle against the class enemies, or tales of Mao's revolutionary heroes. There were also popular opera and ballet movies.

As soon as a date was set and the names of the movies were known, we would discuss nothing but the coming event. I could hardly contain my excitement! I was such an emotional mess at the movies. *Everything* would make me sob. My devotion to Mao and his ideology was greatly intensified. I wanted to be a revolutionary hero! But I loved the Beijing Opera singers as well, their singing, dancing, fighting, and acrobatic skills. They were as close to a kung fu movie as we would ever get. The kung fu masters were the heroes of my imagination, but kung fu books and movies were banned in China then. Only the folktales told by some of the elderly villagers kept that passion alive.

I liked the fighting in the Chinese ballet movies, but I really thought the people looked funny standing on their toes, and they didn't speak any words. Opera always won over ballet when we chose a play to act out.

Secretly I held a dream—one day I would be able to sing and do the kung fu steps of the opera singers. But I knew deep in my heart that this dream would never come true. My future lay in the commune fields as a laborer.

SEVEN

# Leaving Home

I was nearly eleven years old when the headmaster came into our freezing classroom with four dignified people.

I immediately thought of the incident about the writing on the wall. What was wrong this time? But to my surprise, the headmaster introduced them as Madame Mao's representatives from Beijing. They were here to select talented students to study ballet in Beijing and to serve in Chairman Mao's revolution. He asked us all to stand up and sing "We Love Chairman Mao":

The east is red, the sun is rising.
China's Mao Zedong is born.
Here to give us happiness.
*Hu lu hai ya.*
Our lucky star who saved us all.

As we sang, the four representatives came down the aisles and selected a girl with big eyes, straight teeth, and a pretty face. They passed me without taking any notice, but just as they were walking out of our classroom, Teacher Song hesitated. She tapped the last gentleman from Beijing on the shoulder and pointed at me. "What about that one?" she said.

The gentleman from Beijing glanced in my direction. "He can come too," he said in perfect Mandarin dialect.

The girl with the big eyes and I followed Madame Mao's people into the headmaster's office.

There were eight other children already in the room when we arrived. We all wore our thick, quilted homemade coats and pants and looked like little round snowballs.

"Take all your clothes off except your underwear! Step forward one by one! We are going to measure your body and test your flexibility," a man wearing glasses ordered.

Everyone stood there nervously. Nobody moved.

"Didn't you hear? Take your clothes off!" our headmaster barked.

"I'm sorry," one of the boys answered timidly. "I don't have any underwear."

To my surprise, I was the only child who had underwear, hand-me-downs from several older brothers, patchworked with mending by my niang. All ten of us during that audition had to share my one set of underwear.

The officials measured our proportions: upper body

and legs, neck length, even our toes. I watched the students being tested before me; they cried out and winced. One of the officials came over to me and bent both my legs outward. Another official held my shoulders to stabilize me and a third pushed his knee against my lower back, at the same time pulling both my knees backward with great force to test the turnout of my hip joints. It was so painful I wanted to scream, but for some reason I didn't. I had a stubborn thought: I didn't want to lose my dignity, I didn't want to lose my pride. I clenched my teeth.

By the time they'd finished testing everyone, only one boy and one girl were selected to go to the next level. I was that boy. I was excited but frightened. The officials mentioned ballet; but I had no idea what ballet was all about.

The audition was a hot discussion topic in our village over the next few days. At first my parents didn't pay much attention. There was no way in the world anyone in our family could have any artistic talent. My brothers and classmates teased me. "Show us a ballet step! Show us a ballet step!" They knew I had no idea. For me, the most exciting aspect of it all was not the ballet but the possibility of going to Beijing to be near our beloved Chairman Mao: the possibility, however unlikely, of getting out of my deep well.

I went to the commune office a few weeks later to go through the next level of audition. This was much harder. The girl with the big eyes from my class didn't pass this round: she screamed when they bent her body backward and was disqualified. Then it was my turn. One teacher lifted one of my legs upward, two others held my other leg steady and straight. They kept asking me if it hurt. It was excruciating! But I was determined to be chosen, so I kept smiling and replied, "No, it doesn't hurt," as they lifted my leg higher and higher. *Be strong! Be strong! You can bear the pain!* I kept telling myself. I did bear the pain, but the hardest thing was pretending to walk normally afterward. They had torn both my hamstrings.

After the audition at commune level we went through to county, city, and provincial levels. Each time more children auditioned and more were eliminated. During the physical examination at the county level, the scar on my arm from the burn I received as a baby nearly disqualified me. One of the teachers from Beijing noticed it and referred me to a medical examiner.

"How did you get this scar?" the doctor asked.

I didn't want anyone to think of my niang as irresponsible, so I told him I'd cut my arm on a piece of broken glass and that the cut had got infected.

"Do you have any funny sensations, like itching on rainy days?"

"No, never." I looked straight into the doctor's eyes. I prayed he wouldn't eliminate me. I prayed for my niang's sake. She would feel so guilty if I was disqualified because of this scar. After the examination, I overheard the doctor talking to Chen Lueng, the teacher from the Beijing Dance Academy. He was the gentleman from Beijing who Teacher Song had tapped on the shoulder that day at my school. "That boy's scar will definitely get larger as he grows," the doctor told him. My heart sank. My only chance of getting out of my deep well was gone. I made up my mind never to tell my niang it was the scar that did it.

When the physical tests were completed, we were tested for other abilities: our response to music, our understanding of Chairman Mao's ideology. They also checked our family background three generations back. Chairman Mao's communist theory about the so-called "three classes of people" was crucial when selecting us. All three classes had to be represented—peasants, workers, and soldiers. Children whose families were associated with wealth and education anywhere in the past three generations were disqualified. Madame Mao wanted to train us to be faithful young guards. Our backgrounds had to be pure and reliable.

The final hurdle in the selection process was for the officials to meet my family. They wanted to meet everyone to check out their physical proportions. I was nervous they might have a problem with my niang because she was short, but her larger-than-life personality, and my dia's good figure, saved the day.

⁓

Days, weeks passed. No news from Beijing. The hope in my heart dimmed with each passing day. My family had also given up hope by now. I could tell they felt sorry for me, because they went out of their way to be nice.

Then one day, just as my dia was going back to work after lunch, a group of village, commune, county, *and* city officials suddenly came into our small courtyard. My parents offered them tea. Eventually one of the officials turned to my niang. "Your lucky son Li Cunxin has been chosen for Madame Mao's Beijing Dance Academy."

I was stunned. We all were. A whole month had gone by! How could this be? My mother was speechless, but her face smiled like a full-bloomed flower. "Thank you! Thank you!" was all she could say.

My dia poured more and more tea for the officials. His face was filled with pride.

When the officials had left our house, my dia had to get to work. But he looked at me in a strange way, as though he was seeing something new.

After everyone had gone, my niang and I were left to ourselves. She looked at me for a long time, lost for words for the first time in her life. Finally she said, "My lucky boy, I'm so happy for you. This is the happiest day of my life!"

"I don't want to leave you," I said.

She looked at me with a slight frown. "Do you want to stay here and eat dried yams for the rest of your life? My dear son, this is your chance to escape from this cruel world. Go, and do something special with your life!

Become someone other than a peasant boy. Don't look back! What is here? A leaking roof, an empty stomach!"

"Stop it!" I said. I put my hand over her mouth. Happy tears welled in her eyes. She pulled me close and hugged me tight. I wanted us to stay like that forever.

"Can you come with me?" I asked eventually.

"Why? Do you want me to come and wipe your bottom, silly boy?" she replied with a chuckle. "No, I can't go with you, but my love will. I will always love you, with all my heart. I know you have your secret dreams. Follow them. Make them come true. Now, go and play with your friends." She gave me a gentle push, but just as I was disappearing into the streets, she called out: "Don't forget to come back and help me with dinner!"

~⊛~

A few days after this, we received a letter notifying me that I was to leave for Beijing in four weeks, just after the Chinese New Year. For the opening of Madame Mao's new Beijing Dance Academy, fifteen students had been selected from Shandong Province. Fifteen from over seventy million people. Twenty-five students from Shanghai, three students from Beijing, and one student from Inner Mongolia were also selected. It was February 1972. I had just turned eleven.

The whole village came to congratulate my parents. There would be one less mouth to feed and their sixth son had some hope of making a decent life for himself.

Our Chinese New Year was extra special. My eldest brother was home from Tibet. It was a joyous time.

A few days before New Year's Eve, however, one of my "double kicker" firecrackers went wrong and exploded twice in my hand. It nearly tore off my thumbnail, and blood gushed out from under it. My parents immediately worried that this could jeopardize my chances of going to Beijing, so as an extra precaution they took me to the hospital to get my first tetanus shot, an expensive luxury. Normally nobody would have bothered. "Put some dust on it," my niang would have said.

For my last dinner at home my niang has cooked a delicious meal. She's made an egg dish with dried shrimp, and Chinese cabbage with pieces of pork. I can't eat much, despite the good food. My stomach is full of anxiety and dread. I am afraid to look into my niang's eyes: if I do I know my tears will overflow.

As soon as dinner is finished I announce that I am going to my friends' houses to say good-bye.

"Be home early if you want to go tonight," my niang says. "You should get some good sleep in your own bed."

I quickly slip off the kang and go outside.

I have no intention of going to my friends' houses. I just want to be alone. I pass my friends' places but don't go in. "You should be happy," I keep telling myself. And I am, deep inside, happy about this god-given opportunity, but I am overwhelmed by sadness as well. I don't want to leave my niang, my dia, my brothers, and my friends. I can't imagine how alone I will feel in Beijing. I look up at the stars. Even they are few and distant tonight.

Eventually I wander home. My parents have already spread the quilts on the bed and are waiting for me.

"How are your friends?" my niang asks.

"Fine," I reply. I look at her eyes for the first time that night. They are moist.

"Sixth Brother, can I sleep on your side tonight?" my little brother, Jing Tring, asks.

"Yes," I reply. I wish I could put him and the rest of my family in my pocket and take them to Beijing with me.

Tonight, as Jing Tring is sleeping, I look at his content and peaceful face. Suddenly I feel a rush of brotherly affection for him. I wish I'd been kinder to him.

My niang has made me a black corduroy jacket to take to Beijing. I know my youngest brother loves that jacket. In the middle of the night, I quietly tuck it inside one of the papier-mâché clothes boxes for Jing Tring to find after I'm gone.

The morning finally arrives. I wake with the first sound of the rooster's call. My dia rose earlier, to pack my belongings in two string bags. They are loosely woven, so you can see clearly what is inside. Many of my relatives, friends, and neighbors have given me presents: souvenirs or some local specialty food such as dried shrimp.

Some of my classmates and friends have chipped in to

pay for us to have our photos taken together. They also give me a beautiful diary with many pictures of Chairman Mao. The photo means a lot to me. We have only one other family photo—a black-and-white one of my niang and her seven boys. There is also my niang's handmade quilt, a thin futonlike mattress, two small hand towels, some clothes, apples, pears, and a Qingdao specialty called "sorghum sweet." My niang has also packed some dried snakeskin.

After he finishes packing my bags, my dia hands me five yuan. "I wish I could give you more. Be good. Don't let the Li name down." He leaves for work, saying he'll try to make it back for lunch to see me before I leave.

My niang is busy making dumplings this morning, as a special treat to send me on my way. I want to stay with her for every remaining minute, but I can't. I know if we look at each other we will not be able to control our tears. So I walk around the village, bidding farewell to my friends. I ask several of my niang's friends to come to our house after lunch to keep her company. I don't want her to be sad and on her own. I go to my na-na's grave and to our ancestors' burial place and kowtow. I want to smell the earth, the air, to remember the surroundings and take everything in. This village has been my life for my whole eleven years. My heart feels as though it is hanging in midair. I return home for lunch.

My niang has made many dumplings and although they are my favorite, I can't eat even one. A hot ball of emotion is stuck in my throat. All six of my brothers are at the table. I want to say something special to each of them, but few words are spoken. Time seems to run so fast, and it is soon time for me to go. I have to say good-bye.

My brothers take my bags outside. My dia didn't make it back for lunch. I look at my niang for the first time today and we both burst into tears. We can say nothing. We just hold each other. Then some of her friends arrive, as I had asked them to, and I go quickly into the street.

My oldest brother, Cuncia, is to come with me as far as Qingdao City, and as a special honor our village has provided their only tractor to take us there. The admission letter from the Dance Academy said that all fifteen students chosen from Shandong Province are required to meet at a dormitory to spend the night before our train journey to Beijing. As the tractor pulls away from our house, three of my brothers run after us, crying and shouting good-bye. I sob all the way to the city.

The tractor journey takes over an hour. Finally we reach our gathering place. The dormitory feels foreign and unwelcoming. Nothing feels right. I am shy. Already I miss my parents and brothers.

The time at the dormitory allows us to meet the other students. Four are from the countryside, the others from the city. There is something different about the city students. They seem more worldly than us country kids. There is also a man wearing a military uniform. He is called "the political head." And there's one of the teachers who auditioned us. They have come to Qingdao to bring us to Beijing. I have trouble understanding some of their talk because they all speak in the Mandarin dialect.

Before bed, my brother peels me an apple, since I still haven't eaten since breakfast. It's the first time I've ever had a whole apple to myself. I feel so lucky and special. We settle down for the night. My only real comfort is my big brother, sleeping on a small bed next to mine.

Early next morning, we take a bus to the train station, an old building crammed with hundreds of people. I have never been to a train station before. I've only seen trains from a distance. Our teachers push their way through the crowds onto the train, and we pass our luggage through the windows.

I leave my brother standing on the platform and find my seat on the train. Five minutes before departure, the loud-speakers announce that all family members and friends are to leave the platform. This is my last chance to say good-bye to my brother. He extends his hand through the window. As I grasp it I feel him give me something. It is a two-yuan note, his cigarette money. He will have to go without them for the next few months. I know how precious his cigarettes are to him. I hold the money in my hand, tears streaming down my face, and watch Cuncia disappear.

With a sudden jolt, a massive puff of steam swallows our carriage and Qingdao Station slowly slips away. With the *click-clack* sound of each passing section of the track, I know I am moving farther and farther away from my parents. My heart races along with the gathering speed of the train. I don't know how I am going to survive the next twelve months before seeing my niang again.

At first, the trees and fields flashing by are familiar sights, but then the landscape changes and the trees, crops, even the smell of the air, become different. Although it's winter, the windows are open to allow the fresh air in.

At almost the halfway point in the journey, the train stops at Jinan, the capital of Shandong Province. Here the station is grander than Qingdao's, and well lit. Our teachers tell us that we can go and stretch our legs. There are peasants selling smoked chicken, steamed bread, roasted peanuts, sunflower seeds, and sweets. Most of the students from the city buy something but the country students like me just watch.

Later, back on the train, the political head and the teacher lead us to the dining car. Normally only government officials are allowed in this car, but we are Madame Mao's special students! There are two cold dishes on each table, pickled peanuts and some marinated beef. We quickly demolish the cold dishes and then three steaming hot courses arrive: a whole fish, stir-fried pork with green chives, and a mixed vegetable dish. We each have a bowl of rice. The rich and delicious smells take my breath away. Every dish is shining with oil! I have never seen so much meat in my whole life! We devour the food like hungry tigers.

I hardly sleep for the entire twenty-four hours of the train journey. Just before we pull into Beijing Station, our teachers warn us that it will be very crowded. Stay very close, or we will get lost, they say.

I am stunned by the sea of people at the station. Instead of hundreds of people, I see hundreds of thousands, all pushing and shoving in a huge open space. Even the passageways are chock-a-block with people, sleeping on the floor while they wait for their train. The sound is deafening. And the smell is indescribably strange—virtually everyone carries some kind of hometown delicacy. I have my apples, pears, sorghum sweets, snakeskin, and dried shrimps, but who knows what others are carrying? I want to escape from this place as quickly as I can, but my bags are too heavy and I can only move slowly. I try hard to keep up with my group. I enter a tunnel, but when I come out the other end, my fellow students are nowhere in sight. I look around. I don't know which direction to take. Exhausted and desperate, I move to the side and sit down against a wall, lost.

I'm frightened. I want to go home to my niang. I start to sob. A soldier asks me why I am alone. I tell him I'm lost, and he kindly takes one of my bags and leads me to the exit. I am so grateful to him, and as I step out of the crowded train station I am relieved to see one of our teachers from the Dance Academy.

It is Chen Lueng, the tall teacher who auditioned us. A bus from the academy is waiting too—I'm the last person to climb on.

I hear one of the teachers tell the driver to close the door. I want to be helpful, so I start to pull the door closed, but the driver has pushed the control button and the door closes automatically in front of me. It takes me by total surprise. The old-fashioned buses at home don't have doors like this. I stumble back and fall. Everyone laughs. I have made a fool of myself within the first few minutes of being in Beijing.

Throughout my childhood in Qingdao, I'd always lived with the harsh reality of not having enough food, seeing my parents struggle, witnessing people dying of starvation. I would have sacrificed my own life to help my family, but would that have made much difference?

Yet somewhere deep in my heart there is a buried seed of hope. That seed has always existed, and its power is strong. It makes me feel that one day everything will be all right.

Beijing is my chance. I was scared to leave my parents, yet I knew this would be my only chance of helping them. I am afraid of what is waiting for me, yet I know I have to take that first step forward. I can't let my parents down. I can't let my brothers down. I am carrying their dreams as well as my own. My niang said "never look back."

I pick myself up off the floor of the bus and walk down the aisle toward my seat.

# PART TWO

## Beijing

EIGHT

# Feather in a Whirlwind

At first the thrill of being in Beijing near our beloved leader Chairman Mao completely overwhelmed me. Here I was, part of the Beijing Dance Academy, with Madame Mao our honorary artistic director. My family, the people in our village and commune, even the Shandong Province officials would all have enormous expectations of me: from this moment onward, I would have an "iron rice bowl"—a good job and enough food for life.

On the way to our academy on the bus that day, we detoured to Zhongnanhai, where Chairman Mao, Madame Mao, and all the top government officials lived: a huge complex, close to the Forbidden City, with barbed wire and high, faded red-gold walls. Security guards stood beside huge red doors, their hands firmly grasping semi-automatic guns. Guards seemed to be everywhere, spread evenly along the walls. I simply couldn't *believe* I was here! Here, where our godlike leader slept, worked, and made all his important political decisions.

I was stunned with the sheer scale of Beijing: enormous buildings, wide smooth streets, nothing like the muddy dirt roads we had in Laoshan County. And the men and women—their Mao-style jackets looked so smart! I could see very few patches on their clothes. And the number of cars, buses, jeeps, bicycles—how could there be so many bicycles in one city! Officers in army uniforms directed the flow of traffic, but nobody seemed to pay much attention to the traffic lights.

As the bus pulled into Tiananmen Square, my heart leaped. I immediately noticed the Gate of Heavenly Peace on our left and the grand building of the People's Congress on the right. I'd seen them in so many pictures. Tiananmen Square was our great symbol of communism. It was here, at the Gate of Heavenly Peace, that Chairman Mao declared the birth of the People's Republic of China on October 1, 1949, a date that all the children of China had etched into their minds.

We got out of the bus and our political heads and teachers herded us toward the Gate of Heavenly Peace. People swarmed everywhere. Then one of our political heads told a security guard that we were from Madame Mao's school. That mention was enough; he let us into the security area surrounding the Gate of Heavenly Peace, so we could pose for several group photos.

Back on our bus, a sense of insecurity began to overwhelm me. I sank down into my seat and looked out of the window. The buildings around the Square seemed to stare at me. Why are *you*, peasant boy, here in this magnificent city? Here among fifteen million people, I felt like a feather swept up in a whirlwind.

We traveled through the city streets and gradually the tall buildings of Beijing were left far behind. We drove on, heading toward a village called Zhuxingzhuang, about 118 miles away, which was to be our new home.

The wide, open fields of the countryside seemed flat compared to the terraced fields surrounding my home town, but there were enough similarities in the countryside to relieve my anxiety a little. We sang propaganda songs as we went along and this helped me too. Eventually, just as our bus turned into a drive, the political head proudly announced, "We are here!"

I could see tall, bare trees on each side of a driveway that led to a metal-barred gate, which had bright red letters over the top: CENTRAL 5-7 PERFORMING AND ARTS UNIVERSITY. The numbers, our political heads explained, referred to May 7, 1970, when Madame Mao delivered a famous speech encouraging all intellectuals to engage, both physically and mentally, with the three classes: peasants, workers, and soldiers. The Ministry of Culture then proposed that Madame Mao should be the artistic director of this new university, and that it should be located in the heart of the communes, where future artists could learn and work among the peasants every day. In this isolated site, students would be protected from any negative city influences. The project quickly received the central government's backing.

Our bus came to a stop inside a compound and we were all taken inside a new three-story building with an overpowering smell of fresh paint. Before we climbed upstairs, one teacher divided us into groups according to age and gender. I was put in the younger boys' class.

There were two bathrooms, one for each sex. We were told we had to collect our hot water from the boiler-room near our canteen. Water coming through pipes, instead of having to carry buckets from the well. Amazing!

There were four rooms, two for boys and two for girls, with about ten of us to a room. The beds were crammed close together. It would be a luxury to have a bed all to myself, but I knew I'd still miss my brothers' smelly feet and long for the security of my parents' presence.

I put my snakeskin and the smelly dried shrimp and other items in a little bedside chest, got out my niang's precious handmade quilt and carefully folded it on top of the bed. Then we were all taken to the field near the canteen and organized into four straight lines according to height, the smaller ones at the front. I was the second smallest boy in my line.

A broad, strong man in a green army uniform addressed us. "Students, I am Director Wang," he said in a rusty, deep voice. He looked around. I could see his scary little eyes. "On behalf of our beloved Madame Mao, I welcome you to the Central 5-7 Performing and Arts University. You are privileged to be chosen. Do you know what your chances of being chosen were?" He paused. "One in a billion! That's right, one in a *billion*! You are the lucky, proud children of the workers, peasants, and soldiers of China! You will carry Chairman Mao's artistic flag into the bright future. Not only will you receive six years of ballet training, but you will also study Chinese folk dance, Beijing Opera Movement, martial arts, acrobatics, politics, Chinese and international history and geography, poetry, mathematics, and Madame Mao's Art Philosophy."

He paused again. "It is Madame Mao's wish that you don't just grow up being a dancer, but a revolutionary guard, a dedicated servant of Chairman Mao's great crusade! Your weapon is your art. Madame Mao and over a billion pairs of eyes will be watching your progress. The task is difficult. But what you are assigned to do is *glorious!*

"Your parents helped Chairman Mao win his first war. You can help him win his future battles. You will need to work hard every day of the year. Your daily schedules will be posted on the noticeboard on your floor." Another pause. "Any who are not up to this, raise your hand now!" His head did not move but those scary little eyes moved from left to right, and right to left. Nobody raised a hand. He smiled. "Good! Now you can go to your supper."

Director Wang's speech left me confused. I vaguely understood that we had been assigned an important job, that I was to devote my life to Chairman Mao's revolutionary causes. This was nothing new. But I couldn't grasp the rest of what he said about art and politics.

We were led to the canteen, a large room with many tables and chairs. Over a hundred students from the opera and music academies were already sitting at their tables. It was unbelievably noisy.

We were told we were to have better food than other academy students, because of the physical demands of our training. I saw two big bowls of steaming food on each table, and on both sides of the canteen several tables for bread rolls, rice, and soup. We sat down, eight to a table, and divided the food evenly between us. On my table, only one girl and one boy looked familiar: I'd seen them on our train trip to Beijing. The others were all from Shanghai and spoke Shanghai dialect. The boy next to me, as small as I was, turned and said something, and when I tried to tell him, in my Qingdao accent, that I couldn't understand, he just smiled.

The food looked and smelled delicious, but I had no appetite. My stomach felt like a twisted knot. I looked out of the windows. It was already dark outside, and the sadness in my heart began to creep up and overwhelm me. I forced myself to eat a few mouthfuls of rice, then quickly cleaned up and quietly left the canteen.

It was cold outside. The grounds were deserted. I looked up at the distant moon and a few faraway stars in the night sky. I was afraid to go back to the dormitory alone. I looked at the steamed-up windows of the canteen and knew that I couldn't go back there either: they would surely laugh at me. I thought of my parents and all my brothers back home, and with each step toward our dormitory building, I fought my fear and growing loneliness.

The building was pitch-black. I searched for the light switches but couldn't find any. Slowly I felt my way up the stairs and got to my room, dived onto my bed, and grabbed the precious quilt my niang had made for me. I plunged my face into it and wept.

I remember that first night alone so well. My niang's quilt was like a life-saving rope in the middle of an ocean of sadness. I couldn't stop thinking of my family back home. It would be their evening playtime now: my dia's simple stories, my niang's sewing, and my brothers' game of finding words in the wallpaper. I tried to tell myself to stop thinking like this, but I couldn't stop this unbearable homesickness. For many nights in those first few months I cried myself to sleep. I was only vaguely aware of my classmates returning from their supper. I pretended to be asleep and buried my head under my niang's quilt.

The next morning, I was jolted back to reality by the harsh

sound of the wake-up bell. The familiar smell of the smoke as my niang cooked breakfast was not there.

There seemed to be loud bells for everything. Strict orders, schedules, and rules had to be rigidly observed. We'd been woken at half past five. We rolled our blankets military-style and brushed our teeth (I had to watch the others to see how they did this). The bell rang again within five minutes to call us outside onto the still dark field.

We soon discovered that every morning would be the same. Each class captain would report that all students were accounted for, and we'd jog for half an hour around the open fields, half-asleep. I loved the fresh morning air but at first I found it hard to wake up so early. Breakfast was at seven-fifteen: rice porridge, steamed bread, and salty pickled turnips. Never dried yams! Sometimes we even had eggs.

That first morning after breakfast we went to try on our white vests, dark blue shorts, and bright blue cotton tracksuits. The dark blue shorts had elastic on the waist and around each leg. They felt strange. Then we were introduced to Chiu Ho, the head ballet mistress, who took us to the shoe workshop for our ballet-shoe fittings.

In the shoe workshop, Chiu Ho told us to choose the tightest ballet shoes possible, because they would eventually stretch. We were then greeted by a short hunchbacked man who was supposed to be the best maker of ballet shoes in China. His workshop had racks and racks of ballet shoes, including pointe shoes. There were stacks of leather and cotton fabrics and buckets full of shoe glue. A few sewing machines sat on workbenches against the walls. Then my eyes fixed on the rows of pointe shoes. I immediately feared the time when I would have to squeeze my feet into these tiny, tiny shoes.

"Boys first!" Chiu Ho barked. One by one we tried on the ballet shoes. They were so small they cramped my long toes. I couldn't imagine how uncomfortable the hard, tiny pointe shoes would be.

"Okay, boys are done! You can all get out of here!" Chiu Ho bellowed.

"What about the pointe shoes?" I asked.

"What about them?" She frowned.

"Don't we have to try them on?" I asked.

She and the shoemaker roared with laughter. "Only girls wear pointe shoes!" Chiu Ho chuckled.

I felt like collapsing with relief! I didn't realize that even the small flat shoes Chiu Ho had given me to wear would be enough to cause permanent damage to my toes.

We spent the rest of that day preparing for the official start of our training. The Beijing Dance Academy, we were told, was regarded as the most prestigious dance school in the whole of China. Madame Mao's military officers headed key departments of the university. These were the "political heads" we had already encountered, and we soon learned to be terrified of them too. Even our teachers seemed to show them an unusual amount of respect. They had absolute power and would become our political and ideological mentors.

We checked our timetable. Classes would begin the following morning. Our first class was ballet, followed by Beijing Opera Movement and Chinese folk dance. We would do ballet every morning; other classes alternated on different days. Lunch was at noon. Between 12:30 and 2 p.m. we would have our midday nap, a Chinese tradition, and from 2 to 5:30 we'd study normal school subjects such as mathematics, Chinese, history, geography, and politics. Five thirty was dinner time, and for two hours after that we were expected either to study politics or practice ballet.

My first ever ballet class was at eight o'clock the next morning. It was taught by Teacher Chen Lueng, the tall man from Beijing who'd auditioned us at my school in Qingdao.

The studio we were taken to seemed huge and empty with only ten boys and a pianist in it. It was snowing outside and the windows were frosty. There were some heaters along the walls, but they were very inefficient. We wore our little shorts and vests and shivered with cold.

Chen Lueng gathered us in a semicircle. "Can anyone tell me what ballet is?"

We just looked at each other.

He smiled gently. "Ballet is an art form that originated from dancing in the French imperial courts. It is a universal art form today." He told us that our syllabus would be based on the famous Vaganova method from Russia, which had produced some of the world's finest dancers, including Rudolf Nureyev and Vladimir Vasiliev.

Everything he said went in one ear and straight out the other. Those names didn't mean anything to me.

"The first two years are considered crucial. I'll be your teacher for this period. To start with, I'll teach you some basic positions and exercises. Over the course of this first year, I'll also teach you some ballet terminologies. They are in French. The French gave all the steps and movements names, and these are used internationally. It is Madame Mao's wish, however, that we should also give the steps Chinese names. I expect you to remember both."

I couldn't believe what I'd heard. *French*? I had enough problems understanding Chen Lueng's Mandarin.* But I had to think of some way to remember the ballet terms, so when Chen Lueng started talking about the French word *tendu*, I immediately thought of the Chinese sounds *Ton Jiu*, which means "nine pieces of lollies" backward. For *penché* I thought of *Pong Xie*, which means "crab." But for some words I couldn't find any Chinese equivalent. Eventually I tried to write the words in a diary I'd been given,

*Mandarin Chinese, in the form spoken in and around Beijing, forms the basis for Modern Standard Chinese, or the national language. It uses four tones: level, rising, falling, high-rising, to distinguish words or syllables with the same series of consonants and vowels but with different meanings.

but my Chinese vocabulary was completely inadequate. So I drew little pictures instead. I was too embarrassed to ask for help. I was afraid they would laugh at me, this uneducated peasant boy.

During that first ballet class I couldn't feel my toes at all in the freezing-cold weather and those tight, tiny shoes. Chen Lueng told us to stand with our feet turned out in all sorts of funny ways—he called them first, second, third, fourth, and fifth positions. It felt ridiculous. I had such difficulty getting my feet to cooperate.

The studio was damp and dusty and smelled of sweat and mildew. The old wooden floor was splintered, and for our feet to get some grip Chen Lueng showed us how to sprinkle water over it, using a metal pot like a watering can.

Everything felt weird in that very first class. We had to extend our arms to the side, palms facing forward, just below shoulder height, while Chen Lueng walked among us, pushing our arms down and asking us to resist him with all our strength. This was to develop our arm strength, so that our arms would look soft, never strained. This was not dancing, I thought. Where were the leaps and skips? How could I possibly suffer this agony for six years? My feet felt so cramped. I couldn't imagine how bad it must be for the girls standing on their toes in pointe shoes.

That first class lasted two hours. I couldn't wait for the bell to ring so I could take those horrible shoes off and let my toes stretch out. I thought about running in the streets in my commune. I didn't want to dance. I wanted to go outside to make a snowman and throw snowballs.

Our second class that morning was Beijing Opera Movement. Our teacher was Gao Dakun. "Hurry up, you're late!" he shouted. "Spread out around the barre! Beijing Opera movements are all about flexibility and suppleness. Do you understand?"

We all nodded, terrified.

"Good, let's start with your legs up on the barre," he said.

I looked at the barre in front of me. It was as high as my chest.

"What are you waiting for? Didn't you hear me? Your leg on the barre!"

I tried to put my leg up but the barre was just too high.

Without another word Gao walked over to me and lifted my leg. I felt a tinge of pain in my hamstring and automatically bent my knee.

"Keep your knee straight!" He pushed my knee down on the barre. "Now bend your body forward and try to touch your toes with your head. Don't get up until I tell you!"

The pain was excruciating.

"Keep your knees straight!" Gao shouted at Zhu Yaoping, the small boy from Shanghai who'd spoken to me at dinner the night before. "Keep your head down!" he told Fu Xijun, another boy from Qingdao. "Now, let's change legs!"

My right leg was in such pain that I had trouble even lifting it off the barre. I quickly glanced at the other students. I wasn't the only one suffering.

When I lifted my other leg onto the barre, I knew what to expect this time. So I started to count. I wondered if I was the only one counting as a way of coping with such agony, until I heard the boy next to me counting too.

Each time, from that first class on, I prepared myself for the worst. I decided I needed to be mentally strong enough to last through at least a hundred slow counts. But if Gao left the classroom for any reason, then the hundred counts would increase to who knew how many. The pain made me want to scream. We would be in terrible trouble if we bent our knees. My hamstrings would often tear, but we were not allowed to stop. We were not allowed to scream or cry.

I hated Gao Dakun and his class. He constantly screamed at us and called us names. He called me "the boy with the brainless big head."

Before our midday nap on that first day, as we were heading back to our room, Zhu Yaoping, the small boy from Shanghai, slid down the stair rail at our dormitory. It looked fun, so I copied him. We ran up the stairs and slid down the rail, chasing each other, until one of the political heads suddenly appeared. "What do you think you're doing?" he growled.

We stood there, hearts thumping.

"You are *never* to do this again! Do you understand? You could break your legs if you fall. This is not allowed in Madame Mao's school!"

There was no fun in this place, I thought. Only rules.

# The Caged Bird

Every morning it seemed that I had only just closed my eyes when I heard the piercing scream of the five-thirty bell. I'd drag myself to the washroom and pour freezing-cold water on my face to drive away my sleepiness. The jogging, early-morning exercises, and breakfast all happened while I was still half asleep. Only my cramped feet, the ballet positions, and the French names in Chen Lueng's class would wake me properly.

We had our first Chinese folk dance lesson, with Teacher Chen Yuen. He was younger than the other teachers we'd had so far and wore a pair of spectacles. He seemed friendly and even told us jokes.

In Chen Yuen's class we got to dance much more freely. I particularly loved a Mongolian horse riders' dance we began to learn. But the best part of this class was the four musicians who sat at the front of the studio and played their traditional Chinese instruments. I loved the passion of their music. I had never heard anything like it. It made me *want* to dance: I could hear the *clip-clop* of the approaching horses; I could hear those Mongolian riders roaming the deserts, and I longed to be free like them.

That same day we had our first politics class. During that class, I heard some baby birds screeching on the rooftop outside. After the class was over I told Zhu Yaoping, who was fast becoming my best friend at the academy, and we climbed out of a small window onto the steep rooftop, four stories high. There we found ten hungry little birds in a nest under a roof tile. They opened their mouths wide, screaming at us for food. Zhu Yaoping wasn't very interested in them—he'd just wanted to get out onto the rooftop. But my heart poured out to the little birds and I gently put them in my pockets. I planned to feed them some of my lunch before I put them back.

Our next class was math, and I put the birds in my desk. But in the middle of our lesson they started to screech. The teacher was furious when she saw the birds, and told me to get out of her class and report to the political head's office straightaway. I was terrified. I thought they would expel me for sure.

Director Wang looked at me sternly. "Cunxin, *what* do you think you were doing? Do you want to kill yourself, to embarrass Madame Mao? This behavior of yours will not be tolerated! You will study the relevant sections of

Chairman Mao's book and write a thorough self-criticism to read to your class."

"I have never written a self-criticism," I replied. "I don't know how."

He looked at me with a tinge of sympathy. "You must write why you are wrong for climbing on the roof and promise you will never do it again. Make sure you use some of Chairman Mao's sayings as the basis for your reasoning. Say that you regret your actions and that this will never happen again."

I wasn't allowed to go back to my class, so Director Wang let me use his desk while he went to a meeting. After many tries I finally completed my first attempt at self-criticism:

My dear and respected teacher and classmates,

I'm very sorry I climbed on the roof, and even more sorry for taking the poor baby birds out of their comfortable home. The reasons for my action were: One. I heard their screams and saw their wide-open mouths. I felt sorry for them and afraid that their parents wouldn't come back and these baby birds might die. Two. I love birds and always have.

*But*, after speaking to Director Wang, I realize this is wrong and I should never do it again! *Why?* Because of the following reasons: One. I may slip and die and this would cause embarrassment for Madame Mao. Two. Our great leader Chairman Mao said in his Red Book: "Study hard and improve upward every day." By thinking about and playing with the birds, I won't be able to concentrate on my studies like Chairman Mao wants me to. Three. If I died because of trying to save the birds, I would not be able to serve in Chairman Mao's revolution anymore. Four. Also my parents won't be able to ever see me again and my niang will die of sadness.

Because of these four important reasons, I promise that I'll never do it again. If I do, I'm willing to let the thunder kill me!

Chairman Mao's Faithful Student

Li Cunxin

"Let the thunder kill me" was a swear word from our commune. But in truth I didn't really believe that playing with the birds would have caused any harm to Chairman Mao's revolution.

My self-criticism passed the test easily, and my teacher and classmates burst into laughter when I read that last line. I also had to stand outside our classroom for a whole hour afterward. "Cunxin, have you fed the poor birds yet?" the boys teased as they walked past.

I hadn't meant what I'd written. I hadn't learned anything about serving Chairman Mao. It only made me realize how much freedom I was being denied. I would never be able to play with my beloved birds again. Now *I* was a bird trapped in a cage.

There were so many different classes to get used to. Despite the bird incident, I liked the math class and I was quick to understand the new equations, but I didn't understand the importance of math to a ballet dancer and I began to daydream. I could hear the Beijing Opera students' voices coming from their studios and my heart wanted to leap out and join them. I thought about the Beijing Opera films I'd seen back in our commune, and I dreamed constantly about being a singer. I was often in trouble for not paying enough attention, especially in the ballet classes.

We had our first acrobatics and Chinese classes. Acrobatics was very strenuous. We had to do handstands against the wall, and exercises like bending backward and lowering our hands to the floor, the ultimate aim being to grasp our ankles. Sometimes the teachers would order us to stay in this position until they allowed us to slowly bend up to standing position again. They also made us do a lot of quick backbends to the floor, ten or twenty nonstop. It's surprising we were not permanently injured. Yet our teachers continued, relentlessly. "What you're doing now is merely the foundation work," they said. "When your back muscles are stronger we'll teach you backflips and front and back somersaults."

Chinese class was run by Teacher Shu Wing. He was calm most of the time, but occasionally he'd burst into a rage because of our laziness. He had elegant handwriting and I enjoyed watching him write on the blackboard. Words leaped out of his white chalk in beautiful dancing movements. He also taught us classical poetry and would discuss each word in tremendous depth. His class was one of my favorites and we were told we had to learn Mandarin quickly, or we would be sent home.

Gradually I began to make friends at the academy. Zhu Yaoping, Jiao Lishang, and I were often in the same group of activities. We were the three smallest boys, and although we couldn't communicate well to begin with because of our different dialects, we managed in the end. Zhu Yaoping was the liveliest and wildest.

For our first Sunday, a trip to the famous Ming Tombs had been organized. The journey north to Shisan Ling took over two hours by bus and I suffered from dreadful motion sickness. They had to stop the bus twice. I felt embarrassed. But I still enjoyed the Ming Tombs. I had never seen so many pieces of jewelry! Rare gemstones, gold and silver, the emperor's and empress's drinking goblets, swords, costumes, and crowns. How rich Chinese history was! I felt extremely proud of China's glorious past. China was truly the happiest and richest nation on the planet.

But even then I began to wonder. If China *was* such a rich country, why didn't my family have enough food to eat? Of course I didn't blame Chairman Mao. It was Chinese imperial corruption, foreign invasion, or Chiang Kaishek's Guomindang regime that were to blame. I was eternally thankful to Chairman Mao that he had saved us. Only he could lead us to greater prosperity and happiness.

A week later another trip was organized, this time to the Summer Palace in northwest Beijing, but just the thought of the bus trip there and back was enough to make me feel sick. I told one of the political heads that I didn't feel well and he gave me permission to stay behind.

I went exploring the university grounds. There was a small orchard on the southeast corner near the gate— mainly apple and peach trees. They were bare at this time of year, but I could just see new shoots popping out of the branches: spring wasn't far away.

To the north there was an empty stretch of land. I was immediately drawn to it and as a curious peasant boy I soon found myself digging my fingers down into the half-frozen soil to see if there was anything planted, but it seemed completely barren. The land was surrounded by a chest-high barbed-wire fence and I could see a row of young weeping willow trees just this side of it.

I ran over to the willows and began to climb one. These trees triggered such sadness in me. I saw the long drooping leaves and thought of my own sad tears. I wondered if the trees suffered hardship and sadness too. I climbed up and sat quietly inside the long leaves, leaned my head against the trunk, and whispered my homesickness and loneliness into the trees. My tears fell down my face just like the leaves of the weeping willows.

I felt better after my secret confession to the trees. This refuge became my secret hiding place.

I wandered back to the canteen just in time for lunch and noticed a boy sitting by himself at one of the music academy's tables. He was a bit younger than me and looked lonely and sad, so I collected my food and walked over to him. "Do you mind if I sit with you?" I asked.

Shyly he shook his head.

I sat down opposite him. "My name is Li Cunxin. I'm from Qingdao, a student in the dance academy."

"I'm Zhang Xiaojia," he said, "from Henan Province."

"Why didn't you go with the others to the Summer Palace?"

"I felt sick. What about you?" he asked.

"I didn't feel well either," I replied. "What musical instrument do you play?"

"No one has been assigned one yet. Our teachers will test us and then decide what instrument we'll learn."

"Did you play anything before you came?"

He shook his head. "They only chose me because of my long fingers—and my parents are peasants. What about you? Did you dance before?"

"No, I've never danced before. I didn't even know what ballet was. I still don't. I just had long toes and a bit of flexibility. My parents are peasants too."

"Do you play badminton?" he asked suddenly.

"What's that?"

"I'll show you, just follow me!"

So after lunch I followed him to his dormitory, where he took out two racquets and a feathery shuttlecock from under his bed. We ran outside and played badminton in the space between the two dormitory buildings for hours. Those were the happiest few hours I'd spent since leaving my family. For once we weren't being judged or criticized. We just enjoyed each other's company. Zhang and I became good friends, and that more than anything helped ease the intense loneliness and homesickness we both experienced.

❧

From the minute we arrived at the academy, we were expected to wash and mend our own clothes. At home, my niang had done all our sewing and washing. I missed my niang terribly. I so dearly wanted to hear her voice, but I never telephoned the village to speak to my parents. I didn't have the money. Instead I wrote letters, but not too often because that cost money too. My parents wouldn't be able to read my letters themselves, but I knew one of my brothers would do that for them.

The first letter I sent home was so hard to write. I desperately wanted to tell them how much I missed them and how homesick I was, but I knew this would only make my niang sad. Instead I told them about the train trip to Beijing and how exciting everything was. I told them I had plenty of good food: oil and meat in every dish! How I wished I could share it with them. I told them I had to wash and sew my own clothes, and that I'd left my corduroy jacket for Jing Tring.

I didn't think this letter would cause my niang sadness, but my second brother, Cunyuan, replied soon after and said that when he'd read the letter aloud, my niang had sobbed.

One of my favorite places in the academy was the library. It was only a small room with just a few shelves of books, mostly picture books—stories about foreign children written by Chinese authors. These were always sad and tragic. Most were about struggling African American children in America and how the white people mistreated them. Or they were about the struggle between good and evil. The good characters were always beautiful and handsome. The evil characters had big crooked noses and fat ugly faces. They were Chiang Kaishek's Guomindang officers and spies, or the foreign enemies. I hated the evil guys and felt so sad for those impoverished children. I felt even more grateful for the heavenly life that Chairman Mao had given us. If *our* life was heavenly, I thought, then those poor children's lives in America must be hell indeed.

TEN

# That First Lonely Year

Even though those first few weeks at the Beijing Dance Academy were an agony of loneliness, I knew I had no choice but to stay in Beijing. My parents, my brothers, relatives, friends, my old school teachers and classmates, my village and commune, all of their wishes and expectations made it impossible for me to go back. The loss of face would be unbearable. It would damage my family's reputation forever. My success was my parents' only hope of breaking that vicious cycle of poverty. I couldn't let them down, even if I did feel trapped.

I wasn't alone in missing home. I witnessed many teary eyes among my fellow classmates. The girls sobbed more than the boys. Our political heads and teachers showed more tenderness toward the girls. The boys would be told that crying was a sign of weakness.

The city kids seemed to cope better than the country ones. They were more confident. The Shanghai kids coped

114

the best—they were generally fairer skinned too. The country kids were darker and I was probably one of the darkest. Fair skin was considered beautiful in China.

Our first weeks weren't made any easier when a virus swept through the school. I was among those who had the severe cough, sore throat, and high fever. Naturally I did what my niang would have done—I took out a few pieces of my precious dried snakeskin and wrapped a green onion in them. I offered to share it with some of my classmates, but it was as though I'd offered them poison. I lost a few friends over that, but I did notice that their symptoms lasted much longer than mine.

The toilets were another challenge. I appreciated the idea of being able to flush away the waste to who knows where, but the reality that always confronted us was blocked toilets. The smell was revolting. Toilet rush hours were the worst—in the mornings after waking up, after breakfast, after lunch, after nap time, and the worst time of all was after dinner before the "go to sleep" bell. I would close my eyes, hold my breath, and charge into the toilet.

The toilet might have been one of the worst things about the Beijing Dance Academy, but the showers were one of the best. We were assigned to take showers three times a week. We had to get in early because the hot water would run out. Latecomers had cold showers.

My very first shower was like magic. A teacher led ten of us to the changing room, which had wooden benches along the walls for us to put our clothes on. It was very damp, with a pleasant soapy smell. Massive amounts of steam pushed out into the changing room as the class of students before us came out. Hesitantly I followed the other boys into the shower. I was a little afraid, but I'd once heard some adults in our village talking about this thing called a shower, so I tentatively popped my head under the jets of water. It was wonderful! Warm water streamed down over every part of my body. This was a thrilling experience. I had never felt cleaner. (We didn't know, then, that in winter we would be encouraged to take cold showers, to make our hearts and minds grow stronger.)

One of the treats at the academy once a month was watching documentaries and occasionally a movie. All the foreign films were from other communist countries. A North Korean movie I remember particularly well was about a young man who had lost his ambitions for the communist cause, and a beautiful girl, a Communist Youth Party member, who helped him and fell in love with him. What I enjoyed most about this movie wasn't the politics but the love story. For the next couple of weeks I started to behave differently toward the captain of the girls' class, a pretty Qingdao girl with big, bright eyes. I imagined that if I performed badly enough in class, the political head might send this girl to help me, but the longed-for love never materialized.

Within the first month of our arrival in Beijing, we

heard that the president of America, Richard Nixon, was to pay a historic visit to China. It was February 1972. People in Beijing were jubilant. The government's propaganda machine went into full swing and the Chinese media boasted of nothing else. This visit by Nixon was confirmation that Mao's communism had won the final battle against capitalism. I didn't care about Nixon. I was too homesick. But I did notice that the attacks on America's evil capitalist values by the Chinese propaganda machines eased considerably while President Nixon was there.

⁓≪⁓

The first few weeks and months of our dance training I found impossibly hard. I had no idea what I was doing. I couldn't do the exercises no matter how hard I tried. My torn hamstrings from Teacher Gao's exercises were continually painful and I'd injured my back during the acrobatics classes. I knew I was destined to fail—it was just a matter of time before they sent me home.

One day we were given some exciting news: Madame Mao was coming to our university, in a few weeks' time, and a small group of students would be selected to perform for her. I wasn't included. I was heartbroken.

After Madame Mao watched the specially prepared performance, she said to the officials, "The dancing looked all right, but where are the guns and the grenades? Where are the political meanings?" She wanted us to combine traditional ballet steps with some Beijing Opera

117

movements, so from that point our teachers made major changes to our training syllabus. In the middle of a classical plié we had to stiffen our hands into kung fu gestures and finish off with a deathlike stare called "brightening the presence." We had to prepare these "model" ballets, a combination of Western and Chinese styles. Our university strictly followed Madame Mao's instructions and policies. We became nothing more than Chairman Mao's political puppets.

I knew that some of our teachers were incensed by this approach, but they had to bury their love for Western ballet in their hearts. If they didn't, they would risk being labeled counterrevolutionaries, and be sent to jail or the pig farms. It could cost them their lives.

They knew Madame Mao's approach could never work. In classical ballet training we had to turn our joints out, but with Beijing Opera movements we were required to do the opposite. Ballet steps needed fluidity and softness. Beijing Opera required sharp, strong gestures. But propaganda ensured we believed the Chinese model ballets were the world's best. They were groundbreaking, "uniquely Chinese." Nobody dared to question this.

We were expected to memorize every word in Mao's Little Red Book and relate them to our daily activities. In fact, we spent more time on Mao than we did on ballet and all other subjects combined.

We were rewarded for reporting when a fellow

student's behavior wasn't in keeping with Chairman Mao's great political vision. We were even told by one of the political heads that one brave and faithful young Red Guard loved Chairman Mao so much that he informed the police that his parents had Taiwan connections. Both parents were arrested, and their son was upheld as a national hero.

I too would have done anything for Chairman Mao. Anything, except tell on my parents. I loved my niang and my dia too much to betray them.

Madame Mao also wanted us to spend three weeks each year with the farmers, the workers, or the soldiers. These were called the "Learning Three Classes" sessions. We had to live and work among the peasants, workers, or soldiers and at the same time keep up our dance training. At the end of each "learning session" we put on a performance.

Our first three-week summer holiday was spent in one of these learning sessions, with the peasants in a nearby commune. How I welcomed the wheat and the cornfields, the smell of manure, the sound of the crickets! But it made me homesick too. I wanted to go back to my village and catch my beloved crickets again. I wanted both worlds: the good food of the academy and the freedom of my home.

I was surprised that my classmates from the city had little idea about how to work on the land. I truly believed Chairman Mao was right: if these kids didn't come to the commune and work with the peasants, they would have no idea where their food came from.

We continued to practice our ballet, acrobatics, and Beijing Opera Movement every day while we were living with the peasants. We used wire poles and walls for our barre. The dirt ground was uneven and our ballet shoes wore out quickly and were always filthy with mud.

We slept and ate at different peasants' homes during our stay, but by the third day so many students suffered stomach cramps and diarrhea that the school officials had to call in our academy chef to cook for us.

❧

The weather was still hot when we returned to our university, and now came the dreaded visit to the swimming pool.

"Students who *can't* swim, raise your hands!"

A few hands went up—mine was one of them.

"Where is your swimming suit?" the political head asked me. Everyone looked at my practice shorts.

"I don't have a swimming suit."

"Didn't I tell everyone to buy one yesterday?"

I didn't want to tell him that I couldn't afford one.

He gave me an annoyed look and shook his head. "Students who can't swim, follow me."

He took us to the shallow end of the pool and demonstrated the so-called "frog-style," or breaststroke. Following his instructions, I tried to swim, but my body sank as soon as I started to circle my arms. I kept swallowing water. I looked across and saw my classmates swimming and diving like fish and wished I could be like them.

By the end of that summer I did learn to swim, even though I was still afraid of the water.

That summer was so hot. We had no air-conditioning or fans, and for relief we slept on the floor in the dance studio. In spite of the many windows, it was still difficult to sleep. Mosquitoes would zoom around like little vampires. We slapped about frantically, trying to chase them away all night long.

Throughout that first year I labored through the days with no aim, no self-confidence. I couldn't keep up with the pace. It was too much for an eleven-year-old peasant boy. I felt that not a single teacher liked me. I longed for my parents' comfort and love. There was no one to go to for help. So I pulled myself further inward, desperately trying to stay afloat but constantly sinking.

We'd been at the academy for about nine months when our teachers organized another day trip for us, this time to the Great Wall. Again, fear of motion sickness terrified me, but I wasn't going to miss this opportunity for anything.

It was a windy autumn day. We were given three hours to climb the wall. Its bulk and beauty stunned me. The size of the stones, its breathtaking height into the misty mountains, its endless snakelike meandering—it all made me gasp. I had seen pictures of the Great Wall before, but actually to stand on it, to look upon this incredible human miracle . . . I shook my head in disbelief. "Wouldn't it be nice to see the Great Wall one day?" my second brother, Cunyuan, had once said. Now, here I was, climbing the ancient stone steps and wishing that my family could see it too.

The end of our first year was approaching and the end-of-year exams were coming up. Our possible grades were: excellent, very good, good, below good, above average, average, below average, and . . . *bad*. Tension was high among the teachers as well as the students. I wasn't worried about my academic classes because I knew I wasn't the worst there, but my dancing classes were another matter.

There were four dance-related exams: ballet, acrobatics, Chinese folk dance, and Beijing Opera Movement. Acrobatics and Chinese folk dance were less of a worry, because the teachers were kinder and those classes were fun. But for my ballet and Beijing Opera Movement classes I was scared to death. We had to perform in front of academy officials, students from other classes, Chiu Ho, and a panel of teachers with pens and pads in hand.

On the day of the Beijing Opera Movement exam, sunlight shone through the studio windows. We walked into the room in a line—and upon seeing the many pairs of eyes, I froze completely. My mouth went dry, my tongue felt swollen. It was as though all those eyes were focused on me alone.

We were placed on the barre first and before the pianist struck the first note, I was already dripping with sweat. I panicked. I couldn't remember the dance combinations even though we'd been preparing them for four weeks. It wasn't so bad on the barre, because everyone did the same exercises at the same time and I could follow the others, but once we moved into the center of the floor, we were broken up into three groups.

I was trembling all over. My legs felt weak. I couldn't remember a single thing. I was in front now and had no one to follow. I peeked at the mirror and I could see that others were following my mistakes. Teacher Gao Dakun looked at us angrily. As the exam went on I performed worse and worse. The agony lasted for over an hour.

I knew that exam had been disastrous. I was so distressed that I missed lunch and ran to my weeping willow trees. It was over two hours later when I went back to our dormitory.

When I entered the room full of eyes again the following morning, I noticed our ballet teacher Chen Lueng was standing by the piano, looking very tense. My heart pumped faster. This exam was to be judged mainly on barre work—we spent over three quarters of our class time on it. I didn't hear a single note of the music and I could feel my legs cramping. Chen Lueng had screamed at us all year for holding on to the barre too tightly, and here I was, gripping on to it for dear life.

Finally the torture of those end-of-year exams was over. We waited for our grades. I knew in my heart this was not something I should be looking forward to.

I was right. My highest grade was "below good" for math and Chinese. The rest of my grades were "average," even for ballet, and my worst grade was "below average" for Teacher Gao's Beijing Opera Movement exam, which was no surprise to me at all.

I wasn't the worst student in my class, but with my poor results I was definitely near the bottom. We all knew each other's scores because our teachers read them out, loudly, in front of the entire class. My face flushed with each announcement of my low grades. It summed up my miserable first year. I was convinced that soon Director Wang would call me into his office, tell me I was no good, and ask me to go home and never return.

# The Pen

Our first year was finished. The Chinese New Year holiday was coming up and soon I would see my family again. My beloved niang.

Everyone was excited. The school bus took us on a shopping trip to Beijing to buy presents for our families. I bought one yuan worth of sweets and kept the rest, three whole yuan, to take back to my family.

The last two days before going home seemed excruciatingly long. I was terrified that I'd be called up by Director Wang about my poor grades, so I avoided our political heads at all times. But on the final day, I accidentally bumped right into the very person I'd been trying to avoid.

"*Ni hao*, Director Wang." My face blushed. My heart thumped.

"*Ni hao*, Cunxin. Are you looking forward to seeing your family?"

I nodded, petrified. "Here it comes," I thought.

"Have a safe trip!" He smiled at me and walked on.

What about my poor grades? What about expelling me? I was so relieved. Now I could think only of seeing my parents and brothers.

On the way to the Beijing train station, my heart raced faster than the wheels of the bus. A political head and two teachers escorted us, and again, the grandness of the station and the number of people rushing about amazed me. We fought our way onto the train and settled in our seats. A siren sounded. The train slowly moved off. My heart was already in Qingdao with my family.

Then suddenly I remembered my report card. I imagined how humiliating it would be for my family. It would be the most reputation-damaging, face-losing event in the Li family's entire history! How could I tell my parents that I hated dancing? It was all too confusing. I told myself to worry about it later. I was so tired that I fell into a deep sleep and didn't wake up until three stops before Qingdao Station.

It was still dark outside when we arrived but dawn wasn't far off. My second brother was to meet me at Cangkou Station, one stop before Qingdao, because it was closer to our commune. As the train pulled into the station I saw Cunyuan standing among a crowd of people under the dim light. I shot my head out of the train window. "*Erga! Erga!*" I called excitedly. "Second brother! Second brother!"

He saw me then and started to run alongside the train. "It's *so* good to see you!" he shouted. That joyful image of Cunyuan running by the train would remain with me always.

My dia had walked to work that morning so that Cunyuan could pick me up on his bike. Our ride home together took nearly an hour. I sat on the carrier seat with my legs dangling on either side, my bag hanging over one shoulder.

"How are you?" Cunyuan asked as he pedaled.

"Fine, I'm happy to be home!" I replied.

"Tell me, what is Beijing like?"

I told him about the wide, paved streets and the grand buildings. I told him of the Forbidden City and, of course, glorious Tiananmen Square.

Cunyuan was enthralled. He would occasionally ask for more details, so I told him about the polluted air, the vast number of vehicles, bikes, and the hundreds of thousands of people. When I told him about the food we had, he said, "You're making my mouth water!" Then he was silent for a few minutes as though he needed time to imagine what eating such good food would be like.

"Did you meet Chairman and Madame Mao?" he asked eventually.

"Madame Mao came to our school and spoke to us!"

"Oh, you are lucky indeed!" he murmured.

I knew he was envious and would have loved to have had the same opportunities. Trying to make him feel better, I told him about the blocked toilets, my dislike of some of the teachers, and my homesickness.

He laughed at me for making such an issue about the toilets. "Surely they are better than our hole in the ground at home. That doesn't even have a roof!"

"Worse, much worse! More people pooping!" I replied, and he laughed. Then he asked, more seriously, "Why do you hate your teachers?"

"They are mean and some shout at us all the time."

"Have you ever heard of the saying that bitter medicine isn't necessarily bad and sweet medicine isn't always good for you? Surely if you were good, they would have no reason to shout at you," he said.

"I'm no good at dancing. I can't concentrate when they shout at me. I just want to come home," I confessed.

He was shocked by this. "Cunxin, just look at the color of my skin and then look at yours. Within a year your skin has become whiter and mine darker. You don't want my destiny. A peasant's job is the lowest one can have. This is my first year in the fields and I hate it. My whole body is always covered with mud and sweat and what is my reward? Not enough money to feed myself for a single day! Is this the kind of life you want? Please, don't tell our parents about your homesickness. Especially our niang—this last week, she hasn't stopped smiling and laughing. Please, only tell her the good things about Beijing."

By this time I could just see our village in the distance.

"Niang started cooking early this morning," Cunyuan continued, "so you could have a bowl of dumplings waiting when you arrived home!"

I knew Cunyuan was right about what I should say to my parents. I would keep my sadness to myself.

As we turned into our street, we passed some neighbors. "Welcome home!" they called. Down the street I could see my fifth brother, Cunfar, and my little brother, Jing Tring, waving and jumping up and down by our house. They rushed in to tell our niang I was back. As we came closer, I saw my niang come out. My heart pounded with excitement. She wore the same dark blue cotton jacket with patches on the elbows, an apron, and the same patched trousers as always, but she looked older than I remembered.

I jumped off the bike, and tears filled my eyes as we rushed to each other and she hugged me tightly in her arms. "How I missed you! How I missed you! I nearly died missing you!" she kept repeating.

I was in ninth heaven again. This was what I had been dreaming of ever since I left her a year ago.

My fourth aunt rushed out of her house, hobbling on her tiny feet. "Where is my sixth son? Oh, you are whiter and a little fatter than when you left us!" she said proudly.

We all went into our house then. Nothing had changed. I could smell the ginger, garlic, and green onion dumplings. I was so happy. All my brothers sat around and everyone talked and talked. It was as though we were all trying to tell our stories of the past year at once.

Niang didn't say much, but from the way she looked at me I knew she had missed me terribly. Throughout the day I simply hung around her. I felt safe. I felt loved.

"Don't you want to see your friends?" she asked.

"I'll go later," I replied.

"Did you miss home?"

I hesitated, remembering what my second brother had said. "No, not too much, only a little!"

"That's good," she sighed. "There isn't much to miss back here. Only a hard life!"

Just then a couple of my niang's friends walked in. "Aya! Look at him, he has grown!" one said.

Dutifully I answered their questions about Beijing and life at the academy and then escaped to pay my respects to my relatives, neighbors, and friends, and to spend the rest of the morning playing some of the old games with my brothers and friends. I felt so relieved to be back.

I attracted attention wherever I went in my village. I was a celebrity.

"Did you *really* see Madame Mao?" one peasant man asked me.

I nodded.

He grabbed my hands and shook them violently. "It's a privilege!" he shouted ecstatically.

Later that afternoon, Cunyuan rode on the bike again

to collect our dia from work. Jing Tring and I ran to the intersection at the edge of our village. I was excited to see my dia again, but I was anxious about my grades too and worried about his reaction. I saw them ride up and my dia hopped off in front of us. "You're back!" He gave one of his rare smiles.

I nodded. That was all he said to me and all I needed to reply. I loved my dia dearly and I knew he loved me as well.

My niang had already prepared a special dinner by the time we arrived home. We all sat around the kang and again I explained what my life was like in Beijing and tried hard to mention only the positive elements.

"We can't match the food you had in Beijing but I hope you still like my dumplings," my niang said as she set a bowl of steaming hot dumplings in front of me.

"This was all I'd dream about." I pushed the bowl in front of my dia, because I knew there wouldn't be enough for everyone.

"*Liuga*, can you count how many times you ate meat there?" Jing Tring asked.

"Nearly every day!" I replied.

He was wide-eyed with disbelief.

There was silence.

"Madame Mao wouldn't let her students starve, would she?" Niang said finally.

A few weeks before I arrived home Cunsang had been

accepted by the Chinese navy. He was going to be a sailor on one of the battleships stationed in the Shandong Province area, so we talked about this as well. After dinner I took out the sweets I had bought in Beijing and everyone tasted a piece.

Before bed, when I was alone with my parents and Jing Tring, I handed my dia the three yuan I had saved.

With my second brother now working in the commune, I could tell that my family's living conditions had improved slightly. They still ate the same kind of food but now there was a little more meat, fish, oil, soy sauce, and coal; plenty of dried yams; and, once a week, corn bread. My niang cooked me dumplings not once but a couple of times. Even so, there was never enough for everyone, and the dumplings traveled from my bowl to my niang's, my niang's back to mine, and then I would pass one to my dia. Niang would sigh yet again. "*Zhi, zhi, zhi!* Silly boy, just eat them! I know you have good food to eat in Beijing, but you won't be able to have my dumplings again for a whole year!"

My month at home went by as fast as the blink of an eye. I dreaded going back to the rigid routine of the university.

On my last night home, after dinner, when everyone except me and my parents had gone to bed, my dia handed me eight yuan.

"It's too much," I protested.

"Take it. Things are more expensive now. Our lives are

looking up with your second brother working." Then, completely unexpectedly, he handed me a sealed envelope. Inside I found the most beautiful fountain pen. It was deep blue, my favorite color. It would have cost my dia at least two yuan.

"I hope that every time you use it, you will remember your parents and our expectations of you," my dia said. "I don't know what grades your classmates have received, but I hope you will come home with better grades next year. Let us be proud."

I had expected my parents to talk about my poor grades. I had expected harsher words. But that pen and my dia's few words caused bigger waves inside me than any accusations could bring. He didn't blame me. He didn't accuse me, but I felt I had let my whole family down. I couldn't bear to look at him. Instead, I looked at my niang, but she had buried her head in her sewing. I knew that every time I used my dia's pen, his words would echo in my mind.

# TWELVE

# My Own Voice

This time the train trip back to Beijing was a happier experience, and settling in at the academy was easier. By now we could all communicate with each other in Mandarin. I couldn't stop thinking about my dia's pen, though, and his pride-provoking words. I knew that every time I used that pen, I would feel guilty, because my attitude toward my dancing hadn't changed. I still hated it.

In May that year, Madame Mao visited our university again. This time I did get to perform for her and afterward we all gathered at the playground where she told us to study hard and be good students of Chairman Mao's. She told the university heads that the dance students were technically weak, so additional classes were scheduled, including martial arts.

Madame Mao also ordered a young champion from the Beijing Martial Arts School and another from the Beijing Acrobatics School to join us as model students. They were awesome. I was especially impressed with Wang Lujun. He could master ten backflips in a row with ease and do "double flying legs" with incredible height. But his "butterfly" was the most difficult and exciting step to watch. You had to swing your body from right to left, with head and body at chest height, at the same time pushing both legs up in the air in a fanning motion. It looked just like a butterfly flying in the air. He could do thirty-two of them in a row!

Although Lujun was good at acrobatics, martial arts, and Beijing Opera Movement, he struggled hard at ballet. The way the muscles were used in ballet was so different from the way they were used in martial arts. He told me many times that he wished he could go back to martial arts again. Like me, he felt trapped by duty and there was no way back.

Lujun was nicknamed the "Bandit," and he liked it so much that the name stuck. One day he bought ten fen worth of sweets: his father often sent him spending money and he would occasionally slip a sweet or two into my hand. This time his class captain found out and told the head teacher. The Bandit was ordered to write three self-criticisms. He dug deep, but he couldn't think of a single reason why he *shouldn't* buy sweets. So I gave him two ideas. The ten fen he'd spent on sweets could have saved someone from starvation. Or his selfish action could corrupt his mind. I didn't really believe this, but I had to convince him that it was the only way to get him out of trouble. Fortunately, his self-criticism passed the test.

After that incident, the Bandit and I became good friends. To my surprise, he asked me to become his blood brother, a tradition from the kung fu masters' era and a bond that would last a lifetime. I had six brothers already. I didn't need another. So I said no. The Bandit was very disappointed. The following Sunday, he invited me to go out. We got permission to leave the academy and went to a small restaurant at the base of a mountain on the outskirts of Beijing. The Bandit ordered a small plate of pig's head meat, white, and full of lard. Delicious!

After we'd finished, the Bandit took out a small knife, a piece of paper, and a pen. He asked me once again to be his blood brother.

I thought carefully, then told him my real fear: that I couldn't live up to his expectations. I took my six brothers for granted. I had never considered how best to be a good brother.

Eventually I relented. We cut our fingers, dropped some blood into a cup of rice wine, and shared the same drink together. We then made up a poem. Life at the academy was so lonely and tough, the only thing we had was friendship.

That year, the different academies in our university selected even more students. Our complex wasn't big enough to accommodate them all, so Madame Mao ordered each

We spent very little time on international geography and no one took this class seriously, but I wanted to know about the other countries, even though I had to hide my interest. Our history class also dwelt mainly on China, but here I found the rise and fall of the different Chinese dynasties fascinating, especially the Tang and Ming dynasties with their great art, crafts, medicine, and poetry.

We had a new female teacher, Chen Shulian, for our politics class but we studied only communist history and Mao's political ideas. We were starved for knowledge from anywhere outside China. We learned a little about famous communists such as Marx, Engels, Lenin, and Stalin, but only as a backdrop to Mao's great political achievements. Chen Shulian told us Mao "is leading us to the first stage of communism. Where there will be no starvation, no class distinction, no need to work long hours. Total equality. Everyone will work willingly and share equally. There will be no greed or laziness, no cheating or unfairness. We will have the best of everything. Total happiness!"

Chen Shulian's vision gave us a reason to bear our present harsh conditions. She portrayed Chairman Mao as the greatest political strategist ever. It was uninspiring to me but I felt this was an important class if I wanted to become a true communist of tomorrow.

That year I met a new student, Chong Xiongjun, from one of the outer suburbs of Beijing. He was a tall boy, two years

older than me. One day he asked me if I'd like to spend a Sunday with his family.

That afternoon I went to one of our political heads to ask permission to go to Chong Xiongjun's home. He said that my parents would have to write a letter to the academy. The academy couldn't take responsibility if something should happen to me, and even if my parents did give their permission, I would only be allowed to go once a month.

A reply from my parents took three weeks by the slow Chinese post. It arrived at last, written by my second brother, Cunyuan. My niang was happy that I would have a family close by to visit.

It turned out to be the best Sunday I'd had since leaving home. The Chongs made me feel like I was a member of their own family. Before I left, Xiongjun's mother handed me a small bag of dates. "You will come back again, won't you?" she asked, holding my hand tight.

I nodded in delight.

Along with the Bandit, Xiongjun became one of my closest friends. I formed a strong relationship with each member of the Chong family, and continued to visit them regularly throughout the next few years. They became my unofficial adopted family.

I went home to my own family in Qingdao for the Chinese New Year. This time I went with much improved grades. Chinese New Year had always been my favorite time of the

year; now it was even more special because it was my one chance to see my family and friends again. My family could never visit me in Beijing. Just one return train ticket was equal to half my dia's salary for a whole month.

I brought back some Beijing candy and a bag of jasmine tea from the Chongs as gifts to my family.

My holiday month at home went by too fast. My parents and brothers showered me with love and affection. Their lives hadn't changed much from the year before. A few days before I was to leave for Beijing, my parents made Cunyuan write a "thank you" letter to the Chongs to express their appreciation. Cunyuan had to rewrite it several times because my parents weren't satisfied with the words he used. Eventually, an argument broke out between Cunyuan and my parents, and many years of bitterness emerged from Cunyuan's heart. "Cunxin is our family's crown jewel! *He* is allowed to pursue a future. Why won't you let *me* go to Tibet?"

Cunyuan raged with anger, and our niang was sobbing. She knew that they couldn't afford to let Cunyuan go to Tibet. Then Cunyuan fled in anger and despair and didn't come home for two days.

"You are the luckiest person with enough food to fill your stomach," my tearful niang told me afterward. "Never forget where you come from," she said. "Work hard and make a life of your own. There is nothing here except starvation and struggle!"

On my last morning at home everyone was quiet at breakfast. "Take care, be good. Listen to your teachers. See you next year," my dia said to me before he left for work. Soon after, Cunyuan rode off on Dia's bike and told me he would be back in time to take me to the train station.

Nearly two hours later he finally arrived home and handed me a small brown paper package. "You can open it when you're on the train," he said.

I recognized the wrapping paper from the only county department store and I knew how far he had ridden to get there and back.

When it was time for me to leave, my niang walked outside to the gate with us. "Write as soon as you arrive or I'll be worried!" she said. Tears welled in her eyes.

I sat on the back seat of my dia's bike and waved at my niang, at my brothers, relatives, and neighbors. Once we were on the open road, I asked Cunyuan how he was. But I could see his emotions were like a rough sea.

"Why me?" he said. "Why do we have to live in this world? There is no color in this life! I work in the fields every day, in the burning sun, in the rain, in the freezing snow. No days off. My dreams are the only comfort I have, and most of those are nightmares. There is no end to this suffering!"

I tried to comfort him, but in the end I was speechless, silenced by his despair.

We arrived at the station and soon the rattling train

slowly rolled toward our platform. A couple of my friends popped their heads out of the windows looking for me, and my brother passed my bag in to them.

It was time to part. I wanted to hug him but I couldn't— it wasn't something you did with the opposite sex in China, let alone the same sex. "I'm going now," was all I said as we shook hands.

As the train moved away I stuck my head out the window and waved. He stood there until we moved out of sight.

I squeezed onto the bench seat beside my friends and answered their questions about my holidays, but my brother's aching voice kept echoing in my ears. Suddenly I remembered the parcel he'd given me. I took it out and untied the brownish strings. It was a box of candy with a note attached. "*These are for your friend Chong Xiongjun's family*," Cunyuan had written. "*They represent your six brothers' mountain-weight of gratitude and our sincere thanks for their kindness in looking after you . . .*"

This second visit home had made me realize how enormously privileged I was to have got out of Qingdao. For Cunyuan and my other brothers it wouldn't matter how hard they worked. They would most likely be in the same situation, twenty, thirty, fifty years from now.

I knew now, with sudden shock, that I could never go back to the life I used to have. I would always miss my parents' love and my brothers' company, but I knew deep in my heart that my future lay ahead, not behind. This trip home had once and for all stripped away the fantasy of the ideal country life I'd always thought possible.

I fell in and out of sleep throughout that trip back to Beijing. We kept swapping seats so each of us could have a turn leaning against the window, but for the last three hours of the trip I was wide awake. I thought about the year ahead. I was looking forward to facing the challenges. A voice sounded in my ears: "Cunxin, you are privileged. You are lucky. Go forward. Don't be afraid and don't look back. There is nothing back there, only your family's unconditional love that will always propel you forward."

Now, for the first time, this voice wasn't my brother's voice. It wasn't my dia's. It wasn't even my beloved niang's. This voice was my own.

# Teacher Xiao's Words

In the spring of 1974, when I was thirteen, the Beijing Dance Academy was invited to Tiananmen Square to hear our beloved Chairman Mao speak.

This was an opportunity beyond my wildest dreams! I was so excited I didn't sleep at all the night before. I'd only ever heard Chairman Mao's voice over a loudspeaker in our commune or on a radio at the academy. I had memorized so many of his sayings from the Little Red Book; his communist theories were the guiding principles of my life. And now I was going to see and hear him in person! I kept repeating in my head the first words I had ever learned at school: "Long, long live Chairman Mao."

I woke very early on the morning of the rally. It was a brilliant, sunny day. I had extra energy. I wore my best Mao jacket. The bus journey to Tiananmen Square took us nearly an hour. We could hear an extraordinary noise as we got close—loud drums, cymbals, trumpets, instruments of all kinds mixed in with the shouting of propaganda slogans. We waded through a sea of red banners, an ocean of people. It was like an enormous carnival.

The organization must have been meticulous. The police strictly controlled our every movement. Everyone was assigned a location—there was no seating, but packing millions of people into Tiananmen Square took time, so various groups were there to play music and entertain us. The excitement was contagious. Emotions were at fever pitch. This was the happiest day of our lives.

After a few hours of almost unbearable anticipation, Chairman Mao, Madame Mao, and the most powerful members of the Communist Party appeared on the podium of the Gate of Heavenly Peace. Rippling to the distant boundaries of the square, the crowd cheered, clapped, and jumped. The ground vibrated under my feet. Surely the entire world would hear this! Millions of people shouted, "Long, long live Chairman Mao!" Everyone wore red armbands and red scarves. There were thousands of red banners and flags with "Long, long live Chairman Mao" written on them. People sang and danced, eagerly clutching their copies of the Little Red Book in their hands.

I experienced an extraordinary sense of belonging, a sense of being in the presence of some divine being. I was so proud to be a young Guard of Chairman Mao. Tears rolled uncontrollably down my cheeks. I looked around and saw others weeping with joy and pride. It seemed like hours before Chairman Mao gestured for us to sit down and we immediately obeyed.

Mao spoke for no more than half an hour, his familiar voice relayed through the many loudspeakers placed around the square. His speech was constantly interrupted by thunderous applause. We went up and down, down and up like yo-yos, our ovations many times longer than his speech. He spoke with the heavy accent of Hunan, which made it difficult for me to understand him, but I knew that we would study his speech in its entirety over the next few months.

Many hours after his speech we were still in the square, singing and dancing for pure joy.

In the second half of that year the head of the Communist Youth Party at our academy asked me to apply for membership. This was a privilege. Only the most politically devoted students could join. I was flattered and surprised.

I handed in my application and then had private heart-to-heart discussions with three different party leaders. I had to read a thick party manual, full of communist ideals familiar to me from the Little Red Book. Then the committee assigned two members to sponsor me.

After the final vote of all the Youth Party members, five new members, including me, found ourselves standing under the flag of China with the Little Red Book raised by our faces, pledging our allegiance: "I willingly and proudly join the Communist Youth Party. I swear to love Chairman Mao, love the Communist Party, love my country, love my people, and love my colleagues. I will respond to the party's calling and strictly observe all party rules. The party's interests come before mine. I'm ready to give my all, including my life, to its glorious cause. We are dedicated to the principle of bearing hardship and letting others enjoy the fruit of our work . . ."

From that moment on my life had true purpose—to serve glorious communism. Once again I felt a powerful sense of belonging. I took my role as a party member very seriously. I was one step closer to becoming a full Communist Party member, my ultimate political dream. Now I could contribute to Mao's political cause more effectively, and try my hardest to make a difference whenever I could.

But the political situation was constantly changing. Mao knew the Gang of Four, his closest advisers, was incapable of managing China's economic affairs, and by 1974 he felt increasingly threatened by Deng Xiaoping's popularity. Deng Xiaoping's reputation was spreading fast. Within the walls of our academy, however, Madame Mao was still in control.

Madame Mao might have been pleased with our political development but she still wasn't happy, apparently, with the standard of our dancing. The Vice-Minister of Culture sent Zhang Ce, retired principal dancer from the Central Ballet of China, to be the new vice-director of our academy. And Zhang Ce brought back one of his former teachers, Zhang Shu, to be head of the ballet department.

Zhang Shu was one of the founders of Chinese ballet. He had been released from detention as a former rightist—a person suspected of being anti-Mao. He was a small man with an even temperament, and he often watched our classes and occasionally taught us. From the very beginning he seemed to notice me, and I found out that he'd even told Teacher Xiao that I was one to watch.

One day, soon after Zhang Shu's arrival, as I lay on my bed reading, I felt something hard under my thin cotton mat. When I put my hand under it I found a little book. It looked very old and when I flicked through it I saw that it was in a foreign language. I couldn't understand any of the words, but there were quite a few pictures—all of different ballet poses. The young teenagers' ballet positions were beautiful, their figures exceptional. I was especially impressed by a boy posing in arabesques. His placement was perfect. He seemed no older than me. I wished that one day I would be good enough to demonstrate in a book like this, for the next generation of dancers.

I didn't know for certain who had put that book under my mat, but I had a rough idea and I knew it would be far too dangerous to show the book around. Whoever put it there would have wanted me to keep it to myself.

Zhang Ce's and Zhang Shu's arrival at the academy

marked the beginning of our new focus on technique. Extra time was devoted to dancing and some of our academic classes were dropped. Like Zhang Shu, other experienced teachers who had previously been accused of being rightists were now "rehabilitated" and allowed to return. One was a Russian ballet expert who spoke very good English and had translated several Russian ballet books into Chinese. He'd had to do the lowest and filthiest jobs in the countryside; his only crime had been his knowledge of Western arts.

Around the same time, another "antirevolutionary" also came to our academy from the brain-cleansing camps. He was a piano tuner, about fifty years old. He'd been recalled because all the pianists had complained about the out-of-tune pianos. He tuned and banged on the piano keyboards all day long. He took his time and always walked with his head lowered. Perhaps he was afraid that if he ran out of pianos to tune, he would be assigned some other lowly jobs.

The ballet expert was not as lucky. He had to clean floors, walls, and toilets. One day he was assigned to push a heavy two-wheeled cart while some of us loaded it with soil mixed with horse manure. Some of my classmates began calling him "the filthy rightist" and accused him of being lazy. I didn't know what crime he had committed, but after a few trips of pushing the heavy cart I could tell he was exhausted and volunteered to help.

"Thank you, young man," he said quietly. The next day,

during one of our political meetings, I was accused of being weak because I'd felt sorry for the rightist.

"I wasn't feeling sorry for him," I lied. "I wanted to make the process faster so we could contribute more to the peasants."

<hr/>

Later that same year, our academy auditioned some music students from all over China. They lived in a couple of small crowded rooms in our studio building. One of the violinists in that group, Liu Fengtian, was also a good hairdresser. I often asked him to cut my hair. He was the first person ever to use a pair of scissors on me. Before that, we roommates used to cut each other's hair with a pair of blunt clippers. Liu Fengtian was a good violinist who played with real passion. I loved watching him practice. He became one of my closest friends.

In this third year my attitude toward dancing finally changed. For the first time since I had come to the academy I felt confident in my ballet class. I began to do well with our two new, difficult steps for the year: the single tour en l'air and the triple pirouette. With Teacher Xiao's gentle nurturing I made noticeable progress. I worked hard, listened to every word he said, and wrote down my new discoveries in my diary every day. My rapid improvement surprised many of my teachers and classmates.

My progress in ballet also helped me in other classes,

especially acrobatics. Now I was making good progress with backward somersaults, which I had been terrified of the year before. One day, as I was doing one, I thought the teachers were waiting and ready to support me. I was wrong. They had turned their attention to another student. I took off, then suddenly panicked because I couldn't feel their hands supporting me. I crashed down from shoulder height, my back and head landing on the hard floor. I was knocked unconscious.

When I recovered, my teachers and my classmates were leaning over me with anxious, panicky looks. My head and neck throbbed with pain. They carried me to my bed to rest. At lunchtime, the Bandit and Fu Xijun brought me a bowl of noodle soup with an egg in it—a special treat.

No official assistance, no medical care, no X-ray was offered. I was told to go back to my normal routine that afternoon. But my neck pain was intense and persistent.

By the next Sunday I was no better and the Chongs took me to a local healer, who massaged my neck and cracked it with amazing force. A few days later the pain disappeared, but my neck often gave me problems after that accident.

⁂

A few weeks before our midyear exams, Teacher Xiao finished our class late. I was desperate to go to the toilet before our next class. As usual there was a long line. I was late for Gao's Beijing Opera Movement class.

He stopped the music. "Here comes my prized

152

student with the brainless big head! Why are you late?" he shouted.

I had intended to apologize and explain why I was late: to my great surprise, entirely different words came out. "I'm not a brainless big head! I do have a brain!" I stuttered.

"Get out of my class! Get out! *Never* come to my class again!" He pointed at the door, his face red with fury.

I ran to our dormitory and sat on my bed. I was in such a rage that I simply felt like killing him. He had treated me unfairly. He had called me names.

I couldn't just stay in my room—I feared Teacher Gao might report me. I had to act fast. I ran to Teacher Xiao's office and found him alone, reading. I stuttered my way through my story, telling him what had happened with Teacher Gao. He listened attentively.

When I'd finished he said, "Cunxin, I understand your anger and I think Teacher Gao was wrong. He shouldn't have called you names. I will go to Director Xiao and tell her what you have told me. If Teacher Gao goes to her, she will at least have both sides of the story. However, before I go to Director Xiao, I want you to go to Teacher Gao and talk to him. I know how difficult this will be, but I want you to give it a try. He is not a tiger. Have you ever told Teacher Gao how you feel about him calling you names? Are you the only boy he has singled out?"

Teacher Xiao's questions made me think. I wasn't the only student Teacher Gao shouted at and called names.

"Sit down, Cunxin," Teacher Xiao said again. "I want to tell you a story . . ."

One of the guards in an emperor's palace went to his teacher. He wanted his teacher to make him the best archer in the land. The teacher told him to go away. The guard returned every day and begged his teacher to teach him. Day after day, week after week, month after month the guard came. He came in the rain and he came in the snow. After one whole year, the teacher was moved by the guard's perseverance and determination and finally accepted him as his student. The teacher asked him to pick up a heavy bow and hold it up. After a few minutes the guard's arms started shaking with tiredness. The teacher made him carry very heavy loads in each hand every day. After a while, when he picked up the heavy bow again it felt like a feather in his hands. One day he asked his teacher, when would he teach him how to shoot an arrow? The teacher told him that he wasn't ready yet and instead asked him if he could see anything far into the sky. He looked up and looked as hard and as far as he could but couldn't see anything. His teacher told him to look at a tiny little spider in a faraway tree that he could hardly see. He kept focusing on it with one eye at a time. Gradually he began to see the spider clearly and eventually when he used both his eyes the little spider seemed as large as his shield. His teacher said that he was now ready to teach him how to shoot an arrow. Soon the guard became the best archer in the land.

"Remember, Cunxin, nothing is impossible," Teacher Xiao said.

I left Teacher Xiao's office full of hope. I ran to Teacher Gao's office as soon as our next class was finished. He was just going to the canteen for lunch.

"Teacher Gao, may I talk to you for one minute?"

He looked at me angrily. "Better be brief! Come in!"

Once I closed the door he said, "Why were you late for class today?"

"I was waiting to use the bathroom," I replied.

"Why wasn't anybody else late? Are you the only person needing to go to the bathroom?" he asked.

"There was a long line. I'm sorry."

"If you showed as much enthusiasm for your dancing as for the bathroom, you wouldn't be where you are with the standard of your dancing," he fumed. "I accept your apology. Now, go to lunch!"

"Teacher Gao, could I tell you something?" I said.

"What?" he asked impatiently.

"I don't like you calling me the boy with the brainless big head. What if I had called you the teacher with the brainless big head?"

His face turned from red to green and back to red. He sat down again.

"I know I haven't been good at your classes and my danc-ing standard is poor," I continued, "but I was very homesick at first. Now my attitude has changed. I hope you'll give me a chance and judge me by my future work."

He was speechless. After what seemed a very long time he said, "I'm sorry I called you something I shouldn't have. I won't in the future as long as you work hard. Any other issues?"

"No." I stood up and just as I was walking out he asked, "Cunxin, are you going to be able to do your split jumps in the exam?"

"I will," I replied.

I ran down the stairs three at a time. I felt light. I wanted to fly into the air and sing happily like a river bird. I ran to the teachers' section of the canteen and saw Teacher Xiao. I gently tapped him on his shoulder. I smiled at him and he smiled back. We both knew what was meant.

My confrontation with Teacher Gao was the first time in my life that I had really faced a problem and solved it. The problem was like a real tiger before I confronted it and a paper tiger once I solved it. My confidence began to grow.

By the beginning of June, every class was preparing for the midyear exams. The third and fourth years were especially crucial because teachers would select students as their "talents" to spend most of their time and attention on. The exams were always nerve-racking, with twenty or thirty teachers and school officials, plus thirty or forty students sitting in front of us. In this third year, and for the first time in my ballet exam, some teachers began to notice me, especially Zhang Shu, the head of the ballet department. Teacher Xiao came to me after that exam and said, "Cunxin, well done, I'm proud of you. Your diligent work for the past six months has paid off."

After lunch that afternoon, while everyone was taking their naps, I quietly slipped into one of the studios and started to practice my split jumps for our Beijing Opera Movement exam. I had such problems with this step. We had to jump into a split on the floor and bounce right back up again, without using our hands. Half the class could do it and the other half couldn't. I couldn't. But I *had* to. I'd given Teacher Gao my word.

I started to practice. Suddenly I discovered something. Even before I started jumping into the split, my hands were subconsciously preparing to protect me. My lack of self-confidence didn't give my body a chance. So I tried putting my hands behind my head when jumping into the split. My body kept falling to the side, so I turned my front leg out and my balance was corrected. Next I turned my attention to bouncing up from the split position without using my hands. This was far more difficult to overcome. Every time I did it I would feel nothing but pain in my hamstrings and I couldn't find the right muscles to get me up again. I simply had to use my hands.

After many tries I still hadn't made any progress. But I kept telling myself, "I've given Teacher Gao my word!"

The pain in my hamstrings increased and so did my frustration. I was angry with myself. "Stupid you!" I screamed. "Why can't you figure this out?"

I went to the barre and banged my hand on it. The barre shook and vibrated in protest. "Yes, you might be able to help," I told the barre. I held on to it with both hands and did my split jumps underneath. At first, I used my arms to pull me up from the split position. Gradually I relied on my arms less and less. Eventually, I discovered which muscles in my legs were useful and when my hands were finally off the barre I had made my breakthrough.

I was overjoyed. I ran to the center of the studio, jumped into the split and bounced up again, into the split and up. Even the hamstring pain was bearable now. I couldn't believe I had done it.

Then, in my soaking wet practice clothes, I flew down the stairs and quietly slipped back into our dormitory.

In the exam that afternoon, after I successfully completed the split jumps, Gao Dakun's face showed utter disbelief. I smiled to myself in triumph.

My improvements and small achievements over the next few months were like winning battles in a war. I worked harder in all my classes. Teacher Gao treated me with respect now.

From then on my confidence grew and grew. My exam

grades improved remarkably. Teacher Xiao gave me a "good" grade and even Gao gave me an "above average." But I knew there was still much more to do. I wanted to be among the top students in my class. I wasn't sure how long this would take but I knew I would get there eventually. I had the archer's image from Teacher Xiao's fable stored firmly in my mind.

Teacher Xiao also went to Qingdao for a few days that New Year's holiday, and paid a surprise visit to my family, driven by the desire to know his students' families better.

He arrived at our house just as we were about to have lunch. The special New Year food had been depleted and there was no time or money for us to go shopping. Our dia was home for lunch that day and our parents were embarrassed to serve what was left to my teacher.

Teacher Xiao hopped onto the kang and sat between Cunfar and me, legs folded like us in the lotus position. "The reason I came unannounced was so that you wouldn't have to prepare a special meal just for me. I want to eat what *you* normally eat. This way I can truly experience what your life is like."

That meant experiencing dried yams, a few pieces of left-over corn bread, pickled turnips, and sorghum soup. Teacher Xiao started with a piece of corn bread.

"Tastes good!" he said, out of politeness. My niang took this to heart and immediately started to pile pieces of corn bread in front of him.

"No, no! I can't eat this much! Besides, I want to taste *this*—what do you call it?" he said enthusiastically.

Oh no, I thought. Not those.

"Dried yams," my niang replied.

Sure enough, he gagged on the first piece and had to drink a great deal of sorghum soup to wash it down. But the soup didn't taste too good either. I couldn't help thinking it was funny, but I didn't dare laugh.

I showed Teacher Xiao around the village after lunch. He was shocked at our poor living conditions. "Cunxin, you must be thinking about your family constantly while you are in Beijing."

"Yes. I think about them when I'm eating—meat, fish, rice, or fruit. I wish I could help them," I replied.

"You can," Teacher Xiao said.

"How?"

"By working hard and becoming the best dancer you can! I have watched you over the past year and a half, Cunxin. I have no doubt you have the inner strength to become a special dancer. Now I understand where that inner strength comes from. Your parents' strength is in you. It is the most valuable quality anyone can possess. If you are ever in doubt about your own abilities, all you need to do is think of your parents and what they have gone through. Your desire to help them is your incentive to work hard." He paused, with passion in his eyes.

"But I can't do the high jumps or turns," I said. "I have nothing special to make me a good dancer."

"Cunxin, nothing is impossible for a determined human being. Physical imperfections are easier to overcome than mental deficiencies. Remember the archer fable? Nothing is impossible if you put your heart and soul into it! Let's make your family proud! Become the greatest dancer you can be. Starting next year, I expect to see nothing less than the best from you."

From that day on Teacher Xiao's fable of the archer became an inspirational driving force. Whenever I met difficulties or challenges in my dancing, I always went back to this fable for my basic inspiration: hard work, determination, and perseverance. His words had touched me deeply, and I knew that he cared.

# Turning Points

I returned to start my fourth year at the Beijing Dance Academy in February 1975.

Before class one morning, Teacher Xiao called me to his office. "Cunxin, I'm very happy with your work and the progress you have made. I hope you can keep it up. Don't let any outside influences pull you off track." He hesitated for a moment. Then he continued: "I may not always be your teacher, Cunxin. There are people who feel I am not good enough. Some of them have the power to replace me. There's not much I can do." He paused again. I could see he was holding back tears. "All I want you to know is that even if I'm no longer here to teach you, you should continue to work in the same way. I have no doubt you will have a bright future."

My heart sank with shock. I couldn't bear to lose Teacher Xiao! He'd been my mentor, the only teacher in whom I could confide. He was like a parent to me.

"Is there anything I can do?" I asked.

He shook his head. "It's up to the academy officials. Now, go to your class."

I nodded and ran to my next class. But I kept hearing Teacher Xiao's voice. I didn't know what I would do if I lost Teacher Xiao. *I can't lose him!* I kept telling myself.

After lunch I went to Zhang Shu, the head of the ballet department. I felt sure he would listen. "Teacher Zhang, Teacher Xiao is the best teacher I've ever had."

He frowned. "What are you talking about, Cunxin?"

I didn't want to say that Teacher Xiao had told me about his possible dismissal. "I heard rumors from some students that Teacher Xiao may no longer be teaching us."

Zhang Shu smiled gently. "Don't worry, no decisions have been made at this point."

"Teacher Xiao is everything to me! He made me *like* ballet! He showed me how beautiful it is. I'll be lost without him!" I tried hard to control my tears.

"All right, I will take your feelings into consideration."

I left Zhang Shu without knowing if my words would make any difference at all. But as the months went by, Teacher Xiao remained as our ballet teacher.

During that year, Teacher Xiao again worked us hard on our pirouettes and I finally overcame my difficulties. I felt good about myself—now I could always complete three consecutive pirouettes. Then, after class one day, Teacher

Xiao said, "Cunxin, I want to see you do five pirouettes from now on. No more three pirouettes!"

I thought I hadn't heard him properly. "Teacher Xiao, you mean *four* pirouettes."

"No, I mean five," he replied, challenging me. "Don't think, just do it. I would like to see you do *ten* pirouettes one day."

My mouth dropped open. "He must be kidding," I thought. I only just felt comfortable doing three pirouettes without fear of falling. Ten pirouettes was completely crazy.

"Cunxin," he said, "to be the best, first you have to dare to *try!* I don't want you to be the best in your class. I want you to be the best in the world."

Teacher Xiao's words echoed in my ears for days. He was talking about a standard of dancing far, far above me. How could a fourteen-year-old peasant boy think about being the best in the world? But Teacher Xiao's challenge was like a seed implanted in my mind. From that day onward I had an aim and a vision.

That year, our academy was chosen to participate in an important public performance for Madame Mao. We were to dance an excerpt from China's most famous ballet, *The Red Detachment of Women*, all about Chairman Mao's army and its bravery, with the dancers doing leaps and turns with guns and flags and grenades. I loved it.

Everyone was vying for a part. The role of the hero, Chang

164

Qing, a captain of the Red Army, was given to the Bandit. I was among five boys chosen to play the peasant boy, and eventually I was selected to be understudy to a slightly older boy. I was just so happy to be one of the final two.

Chen Lueng, my first ballet teacher, was the rehearsal master for this performance. One day he switched me and the older boy around and I became the first cast. Both of us were shocked. The Bandit was happy for me but I saw the disappointment in the other boy's eyes. I felt terrible. I had taken something precious away from him. I went to Chen Lueng after the rehearsal and told him that I would be happy to remain as understudy.

"Cunxin," he said, "you are better than him and deserve to be seen. If I didn't do what I felt was best for our art form then I would have failed as a teacher. You should stop dancing now if you don't want to be the best."

Deep inside I knew Chen Lueng was right. I knew ballet was an art form based on honesty. The audience could see a good dancer from miles away. I went to the other boy and told him I was very sorry for taking his place.

That was my first career break. Teachers started to notice me more. That ballet didn't just give me a rare opportunity to perform in front of Madame Mao: it also gave me confidence.

This was also the year I started to do better in other classes, especially Chinese. Our teacher Shu Wen, taught us with passion.

One day in his class we were studying a fable that was half a page long. It took Shu Wen a whole week to help us unravel the meaning of the story. It was about a young farmer who had wasted his precious planting season because he'd waited and waited for a blind rabbit to run into a tree and kill itself after another had done so on the edge of his land. "I have discovered the secret of getting food without work!" the farmer assured his wife. "I'll bring home a rabbit every day and we'll have meat to eat forever." But no blind rabbits came. By the time he realized his stupidity, it was too late. The planting season was over and his family's savings were gone.

The essence of this fable left its mark on me. Nothing comes easily. There are no shortcuts. Things only come when one works for them.

After our midyear exams, we started our pas de deux classes. I liked this class—it was our only chance to get near the girls. At first, the girls and the boys were on different sides of the studio. Then we were paired by our teacher according to size and strength. (I secretly wished to be paired with the girls I liked best.) As soon as the music ended we would go back to opposite sides of the studio.

In the second half of that year, some previously banned Russian ballet films were shown to us. We weren't supposed to learn anything technical or artistic from them: we were just supposed to criticize the story. *Giselle*, for example, was clearly a story from a capitalist society. We criticized the pathetic peasant girl Giselle who did nothing but desire the lifestyle of the wealthy and pursue material values. We laughed at her love for the deceitful Prince Albrecht. How stupid she was to turn her back on the peasant who truly loved her. "You can tell this ballet was designed by a capitalist," our political head said. "What a contrast to *our* model ballets!"

We were all Mao's faithful children, and we all agreed with our political head, but I couldn't help admiring Prince Albrecht's brilliant dancing. The dancer was Vladimir Vasiliev from the Bolshoi and his performance left me gasping. Once I'd seen the beautiful *Giselle* I began to doubt *The Red Detachment of Women* was quite so artistically brilliant.

It was during our busy end-of-year exam preparation time, in January 1976, that Zhou Enlai, the Premier of China, died. Several long remembrance sessions were organized to commemorate Zhou's great contributions to China. I was surprised to see so many of my teachers sobbing.

Right after Zhou's death, Deng Xiaoping was arrested. Mao appointed Hua Guofeng to succeed Zhou Enlai but it soon became clear that Hua Guofeng was an ineffective leader, a puppet of Mao and the Gang of Four. The Gang of Four organized a "Denounce Deng Xiaoping" campaign. He was labeled an old rightist whose motive was to corrupt the communist system and eventually overthrow it. Many people only halfheartedly participated in the "denounce Deng Xiaoping" campaign. I could sense a huge tide of resentment developing against the Gang of Four.

Around this time we started to rehearse another model ballet, and this time I was chosen to be the main character. *The Children of the Meadow* was about the new generation of children under Mao and their devotion to his cause. We rehearsed one act of this ballet for several months and then performed it in our academy theater. I received encouraging comments about my performance.

To begin with I had no stage fear at all. But this changed quickly when, a week later, we went to an industrial city near Beijing to perform for the public. During the opening night performance my brain went completely blank. I didn't know what I was doing onstage. I had forgotten the steps. That was my first stage fright, at age fourteen. I would never forget it.

After that performance the head of our ballet department, Zhang Shu, spearheaded a project we began in 1976. We were to create a full-length ballet. The story was about a teenage brother and sister whose parents were captured by Chiang Kaishek's Guomindang army and hanged on a symbolic tree called *Hai Luo Sha*.

I was utterly surprised to be chosen as first cast for the lead role. Suddenly I was the envy of the entire academy. The pressure was immense but the opportunity for me to dance in a new creation was beyond my wildest dreams.

The choreography took over six months. We rehearsed

every afternoon. I changed three to four soaking wet T-shirts every day. My legs started to cramp. One of the choreographers brought me cups of warm sugared water to replenish my lost energy.

There was no doubt this role was technically very demanding. I worked hard but three choreographers had choreographed different sections of the ballet. I had to listen to three people's instructions at once! It was so confusing. The ballet underwent changes right up to the last minute and on the opening night, in front of thousands of eyes, my nerves turned my muscles numb. My whole body trembled. My legs felt weak. On my grand entrance I was supposed to perform this explosive series of giant leaps but my legs felt like noodles dangling in the air. The second half of the ballet went better, but the difficult dancing parts were mostly in the first half.

I was disappointed with myself beyond description. I had let the whole academy down. I had let Chairman Mao and Madame Mao down. I went to all three choreographers and apologized. I went to Zhang Shu the next day and asked him what I could do for my nerves. "Only experience will help you," he said.

~

At the end of this year we spent time with the army stationed outside Beijing. The daily schedule was strict. At five o'clock we were outside in line on the parade ground. We were used to our Beijing Dance Academy's strict

169

schedule, but still, waking up even earlier was hard. We jogged and practiced our morning routine before breakfast. For the rest of the day we joined some of the soldiers' training activities. We learned how to walk, turn, stop, and run the military way. We even learned how to fall and crawl under imaginary tanks and enemy gunfire. Many of us had bruises all over. We learned how to hold guns— important for our political ballets, we were told. We spent days at target practice and my eyes grew tired.

Grenade throwing was one activity I wasn't good at, no matter how hard I tried. We practiced with fake grenades at first. On the day we were scheduled to throw the real grenades we first had to throw a fake one so our throw could be measured. I imagined a group of enemies standing in front of me, gathered my strength, and threw out the fake grenade with all my might. It fell way short of the target. I wasn't the only one—many of my classmates also failed to reach the required distance. The academy officials wisely canceled our real grenade-throwing event.

I didn't enjoy my military experience at all. I spent the whole time longing to get back to my leaps and pirouettes.

This same year I was elected one of the three Communist Youth Party committee members and vice-captain of my class. One day a Communist Party official at the academy called me into his office. "Cunxin, you have done a good job at the Communist Youth Party. Although you are still too young to join the main party, we would like you to start thinking about it now. Communist Party members are the purest and strongest communist believers. The party would like to educate you to become a true Communist Party member, to carry the party's torch. Communist Party members are a glorious breed of human being."

I nodded dutifully and left his office confused. To join the Communist Party was every young person's dream. But when I heard his words about a glorious breed of human being I began to wonder. I thought of the Communist Party members I knew: some were special people like Teacher Xiao and Zhang Shu. But there were others I didn't want to be in the same company with. Besides, with my increased interest in ballet, I had little time for long meetings. Lately I'd started speeding up the meetings I chaired at the Communist Youth Party and I'd been considering relinquishing some of those responsibilities. When I talked to Teacher Xiao and Zhang Shu about this conflict between the endless meetings and my dance practice, both of them advised me not to give up my political position. It was important for my artistic future, they said.

⚘

Soon after Zhou Enlai's death, there was a massive earthquake in the coal-mining city of Tangshan, about a hundred miles east of Beijing. Officially, over 200,000 people were killed and over 150,000 injured. There were rumors this earthquake was an unlucky sign of hard times and unrest ahead. It happened in the middle of a long, hot summer, while we were preparing for our midterm exams. Several older buildings fell down in Beijing itself. Our academy was considered an old building, so we had to vacate it and live temporarily in tents in Taoranting Park. Tremors went on for two whole days. Torrential rain poured down relentlessly. It was wet and cold at night and we had only biscuits and dried bread for two days.

My second brother, Cunyuan, was a volunteer at the local hospital in Qingdao looking after some of the earthquake victims, who came in by the trainload.

Then, in September, the unthinkable event . . .

Our beloved Chairman Mao died.

China stopped. The whole nation mourned. I remember gathering in front of a loudspeaker on the playground and hearing the announcement of his death by his successor, Hua Guofeng. We cried our hearts out. I had worshipped Chairman Mao. I would have died for him. And now he was gone.

The day after we heard about Mao's death, the Bandit and I went to a quiet corner of our academy grounds and sat on a concrete Ping-Pong table to talk about this shocking news. China's future was now uncertain. Mao's death could only mean immense insecurity.

"There will be total chaos in China soon," the Bandit said despondently. "We should be prepared!"

understand what today's world dancing standard is. This is *not*, I repeat, this is *not* for you to learn about the Western world's lifestyle! By watching Baryshnikov, you will realize how hard you have to work to reach this same standard of dancing. Today, we'll show you Baryshnikov's own production of *Nutcracker* and *The Turning Point*."

I was captivated by Baryshnikov. I had never seen anything like *Nutcracker* before. Baryshnikov and his partner Gelsey Kirkland danced to a standard far beyond what I thought any dancer was capable of. But the video of *The Turning Point* totally blew me away. I was mesmerized. I couldn't take my eyes off Baryshnikov. My heart leaped with each one of his astonishing jumps and accelerating turns. For the first time in my life I saw how truly exquisite ballet could be.

From that moment on I loved ballet with a passion. I dared to believe that if Baryshnikov could dance like that, then so could I. This was how I could make not only my parents but also the whole of China proud.

Now I raced through my meals to get back to the studio to practice my jumps. I woke at five every morning. I strapped sandbags to my ankles and hopped up and down the four flights of stairs in our studio building. I practiced my leaps, covering every inch of whichever studio was vacant. I wanted to fly like the beautiful birds and dragonflies; I wrote the word "fly" on my ballet shoes to remind myself of my goals. I embarked on endless sit-ups and exercises everywhere I could find a flat surface and a few minutes to spare. People thought I had gone mad but I didn't care. I had only one desire now—to dance like Baryshnikov.

By the end of my sixth year, after all my exercises, practice, and determination, my jumping ability had improved, but I knew there was a long way to go. It was then that Teacher Xiao started to challenge me with my turns.

I couldn't turn naturally but my newfound inspiration with my jumps made me work even harder. I set impossible goals for myself. One night I went to the studio with a candle and a box of matches. I lit the candle and started to practice my turns. The candle threw only a faint light in front of me. It was hard, but I thought if I could turn in the dark, then turning in the light would be easy. I couldn't risk switching the light on, for fear of my teachers catching me staying up so late. I continued this night after night. By the end of the term there were shallow indentations in the studio floor where I had endlessly, repeatedly, turned.

Many people were very surprised to see my rapid improvement, but not Teacher Xiao. One night, he *did* catch me practicing my turns. It was way past lights-out time. I thought he would be very angry, but he said he wasn't surprised and we kept my nighttime practice sessions a secret between us.

Now I was practicing in those studios five times a day compared to the usual once-a-day routine of the other

*My classmates and myself, center front, wearing Mao's Red Guard scarves.*
*This was taken in early 1972, in Laoshan.*

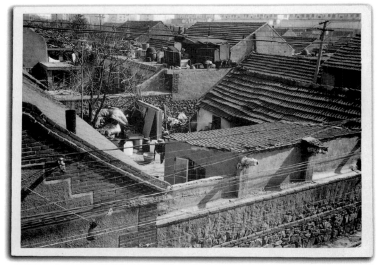

*The New Village, Li Commune—the world of my upbringing. This photo was taken*
*in 2002—nothing much had changed since I was born.*

*Proudly wearing Mao's army uniform, in January 1974— aspiring to become a true and faithful follower of the communist ideal.*

*My beloved niang washing, forever washing, in the courtyard of our home. This was taken when I went back to China in 1988.*

*My first lonely day in Beijing, posing for one of our group photos in Tiananmen Square—I am in the front row, fourth from the right.*

*The Beijing Dance Academy—my world for seven long years. Here it is in 1997—
again, nothing much had changed: the studio building is on the right, hot-water
boiler room and teachers' rooms in the center, and the canteen to the left.*

Hai Luo Sha, *one of our political ballets, with me and "Chairman Mao."*

*Rehearsing* Hai Luo Sha *with Teacher Zhang Shu in 1976. In the background are Mao's grand words: "Have your country in your heart and the world in your vision."*

*First contact with the West—Zhang Weiqiang and I in New York in 1979.*

*On the steps of the
Vaganova Ballet School in
Leningrad—my first trip to
another communist country.*

*Defection. April 29, 1981.
Being freed from the
consulate with Elizabeth
Mackey and Charles Foster.*

*Finally at ease as the Western prince—*
Sleeping Beauty *in 1984.*

*With Barbara Bush at the
White House in 1991. She was
instrumental in bringing my
parents to the United States and
in fostering my relationship with
China.*

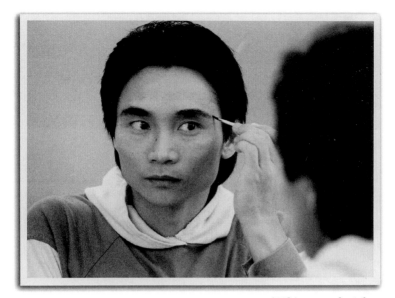

*Applying my makeup for a performance with the Houston Ballet—a new identity, a transformation: what would my niang and dia think of this? I lived in another world now.*

*In Glen Tetley's* Rite of Spring—*making the giant leaps I'd always dreamed of.*

*The* Esmeralda *pas de deux with Mary, in 1990, in a gala performance at the Sydney Opera House.*

*My beloved family in Melbourne in 1997—my wife, Mary, and our children Sophie, Thomas, and Bridie.*

students. "I thought *I* worked hard as a student—I practiced three times a day, but five times is unheard of!" Teacher Xiao said, amazed. Then, more seriously: "Please look after your health. I want to see you last the distance."

⌘

By this time, Mao's chosen successor Hua Guofeng was under house arrest and Deng Xiaoping now became the leader of China. I felt a dramatic change of attitude within the Beijing Dance Academy. Previously, Deng Xiaoping had been denounced for his views. He didn't care which system we used as long as it worked for China.

We had a new academy director, Song Jingqing, who decided that our six-year course of study should be extended for another year until February 1979. We'd wasted too much time, she said, studying politics to achieve technical excellence.

Even by the beginning of 1978 I could feel the real impact of Deng Xiaoping's reforms. He was the first person who had dared to say that to follow Mao's every word was wrong and that the political campaigns and studies must be stopped. Some Communist Party members were skeptical and so were many others. The Cultural Revolution had left such horrifying memories. Why should they believe new policies now? China was unsure.

It was during our last year at the academy that we began to openly practice our art form without being accused of being unbalanced students. Political pressure waned. Selected Western books, films, and performing groups began to appear in China. Getting hold of a foreign book or watching a foreign "colored film" soon became an obsession. We were desperate for Western knowledge. How thirsty we were for foreign literature and how fascinated with the Western world we had become!

Deng Xiaoping's new policy created a breath of fresh air within our academy. The required bi-weekly Communist Youth Party meetings were reduced to one a month. My conflict between attending meetings and practicing ballet was resolved. Political party leaders no longer had the same influence.

For me, this extra year of study turned out to be my best yet. We started to watch old Russian ballet films such as *The Stone Flower*, *Swan Lake*, and *Spartacus*. We saw famous ballet stars like Galina Ulanova, Maya Plisetskaya, and of course Vladimir Vasiliev. We were even allowed to watch that famous Russian defector, Rudolf Nureyev, dancing with one of the Western world's most respected ballerinas, Margot Fonteyn. Images of these extraordinary, inspiring dancers stayed in my mind.

It was around this time, when reading Western ballet books was no longer a crime, that I asked Teacher Xiao if it was he who had left that ballet book under my mat in the third year.

"Did you like it?" He smiled.

"Thank you." I meant it from the bottom of my heart.

SIXTEEN

# Change

Late 1978. Just months away from graduation. On a Saturday night in the biggest dance studio our teachers organized a party. All the senior students were invited.

There were elegant long dresses, and a round silver ball was hanging from the ceiling, spinning out hundreds of different colors and shapes. We were totally entranced. Dancers led their partners elegantly across the floor. Teacher Xiao was the star and many ladies were taken with his style.

After watching the dancing for a while I gathered enough courage to ask a teacher to show me how to waltz. She explained the basic movements, but I kept treading on her toes and apologizing. I may have been hopeless in my first waltz but I enjoyed it enormously. It was the first time I'd heard such beautiful, romantic music. This would never have been possible under Madame Mao's directorship; a waltz would have been banned as a corrupt influence and Western "filth."

181

We began to watch more and more foreign films. We'd devise any possible way to get into the heavily guarded theaters where these "colored films" were shown. Fake theater tickets were made and wigs and mustaches stolen from the costume shops of the academy to make us look older. Once we got into the theater we'd find ways of staying there for the next screening. We'd hide behind curtains and doors, even in the toilets. Anything to get to see those films.

One day the Bandit meticulously glued the torn halves of some used theater tickets together. We whitened our hair and slipped into the crowded theater without being detected. We didn't have rehearsal until three: plenty of time to watch the movie. But neither of us had a watch. "Lujun," I whispered. "How will we know when it's time to go?"

"Don't worry, I have an internal clock," he said confidently.

I was going to say more but the movie had started. It was an American movie about a love triangle. The translated Chinese title was *Hurt Too Much to Say Good-bye*. Two translators, a man and a woman, provided dialogue over a pair of microphones but they often forgot to translate and we were left to guess for ourselves most of the time.

I couldn't believe the colorful clothes the women wore in these movies. So different from how Chinese women dressed. But the high-heeled shoes looked as uncomfortable as pointe shoes. Some of the actresses were breathtakingly beautiful yet they all looked so much alike. It was in this movie that I witnessed a kiss for the very first time. My heart raced. I wondered what it would be like—to really kiss a girl.

The Bandit's internal clock didn't work. By the time the movie had finished we were late for our rehearsal. As we approached the studio I heard Teacher Xiao's voice. My heart immediately sank.

He turned and looked at us, and without changing his expression, went on coaching the other students. I was embarrassed beyond description. I glanced furiously at the Bandit: I wanted to smash his internal clock to pieces.

"Cunxin, come to my office after your next break," Teacher Xiao said at the end of the rehearsal.

I still hadn't decided what I should say to Teacher Xiao when I knocked on his office door.

He got straight to the point. "Why were you late?"

"I went to a movie," I stuttered.

"I had a feeling you had gone to a movie. Although you have told me the truth it doesn't take any of my disappointment away."

"I'm sorry, Teacher Xiao. I thought I would be able to make it back in time for the rehearsal."

He looked at me intently for a few moments. "Cunxin, this wouldn't have surprised me if it had been any other student. I am extremely surprised and disappointed it was you! I don't care if you watch a hundred movies in your spare time but classes and rehearsals come first."

I nodded. I knew I was unquestionably in the wrong.

Then in a different tone Teacher Xiao asked, "What was the movie?"

"A colored film. *Hurt Too Much to Say Good-bye*," I replied, and lowered my head.

"Any scenes without clothes?" he asked seriously.

"No, only kisses," I replied.

"Very well, off you go." He shook his head as he spoke but I could see a subtle smile. I was glad I was honest with him. I could never have lied to Teacher Xiao.

❧

"Colored" movies weren't the only distraction in those last months. I was besotted with a girl from Shanghai called Her Junfang. One night we met secretly in a dark studio. I could sense her unease. I found it hard to breathe. We'd be expelled if the teachers discovered us.

"How was your holiday?" I whispered.

"Fine, how was yours?"

"Good. I brought you some sorghum candy."

"Thank you. I brought you some Shanghai cakes."

We edged closer to each other. Suddenly we heard the door of Zhang Shu's office open and we froze.

To our great relief his footsteps went in the opposite direction. We nervously exchanged our gifts and quickly tiptoed out of the studio.

When I finally sat on the edge of my bed in the dark with Her Junfang's gift in my hands, I hated myself for being such a coward, for not holding her when I had the chance. I couldn't believe that I had forgotten all the passionate words I had rehearsed in my mind before our meeting. We never had the opportunity to get close to each other again.

Other than the Sundays I spent with the Chongs, I used almost every spare moment to practice. I learned more in that one year than in the previous six years combined.

Around the time we were preparing for our graduation the London Festival Ballet performed in China, one of the first professional companies allowed to enter the country under Deng Xiaoping's "open-door policy." They came to perform with us at our academy theater and everyone talked about the "big-nosed people," the foreigners.

I had such problems trying to distinguish one big-nosed person from another. They all looked alike, whether they were in the movies, in dance videotapes, or there in person. I had to remember what clothes they wore to differentiate them. If they suddenly changed costume between scenes I would be totally lost. And they seemed to speak so fast, without any commas or stops. One of the foreigners who came was an eighteen-year-old dancer named Mary McKendry; she watched me dance.

The Festival Ballet performed *Giselle*, and two mixed

programs, including Harald Lander's famed *Etude*. I wished I could watch this kind of dancing every day: the big-nosed dancers' artistic interpretations and discipline quickly gained our respect. I longed to learn more about Western culture, to work with these great choreographers.

Our graduation exam preparations went on for over three months. Our final average grades would determine which dance company we'd get into. The Central Ballet of China would select only the top graduates. Others would be sent to cities far away or to provincial troupes.

A month before our final exam Teacher Xiao came to me and said, "Some teachers think I have allowed you to do too many solos in your exam. Most students will do one or two, one student is doing three. I think six might be too much for you."

"No, I want to do all six!"

"Are you sure? Because once I hand my submission to Zhang Shu it will be very hard to change."

"I'm sure I can do it," I replied confidently.

He thought for a moment. "All right, but just remember, try to find the secret of doing every step as easily and effortlessly as possible. That is what dancing is all about."

The first solo was from Madame Mao's model ballet *The White-haired Girl*. I was to dance with an imaginary grenade in my hand, ducking enemy bullets with fast, crisp movements. But my real passion and love was for the Western classical solos. In those, however, I had real problems with a

186

double *tour en l'air*. To achieve good height as well as complete the two turns down to kneeling position in the flash of an eye was an enormous challenge. My right knee was grazed and bleeding from constant landings. Images of Baryshnikov, Nureyev, and Vasiliev continually inspired me. When I finally got it right the feeling was sensational.

In the end I did perform all six of my solos. I enjoyed every step I danced. After seven years at the academy I had even mastered eight consecutive pirouettes, occasionally ten. And now here I was, one among the last generation of Mao's dancers about to graduate.

For our graduation performance our academy wanted to revive *Swan Lake* for the first time since the Cultural Revolution. It was a difficult task—all the records of Western ballets, including *Swan Lake*, had been destroyed. It was one thing to put together just one solo from a ballet like *Giselle* but quite another to reproduce a full-length ballet. Teachers had to remember details from past performances of many years ago: miraculously this collaboration resulted in the complete ballet being produced. I was thrilled to be chosen as third cast for Prince Siegfried. I concentrated on nothing but my rehearsals. I worked on my weaknesses and focused on my goals, and by the time the teacher in charge of the rehearsals finally decided who was to dance the leading role on the opening night, I had been chosen as first cast.

As I rehearsed my role as Siegfried I asked my friend

Liu Fengtian what he thought of my portrayal of the prince. He said my dancing was good, but I looked like a Chinese peasant boy pretending to be a prince. I knew what he said was true. I had no problem with the dance steps but I knew nothing of European royalty. Even my teachers didn't know how a prince would carry himself. What a prince represented was in direct conflict with the values of communism.

In desperation I watched a few old Russian films so I could study a prince's walk, the way he held his arms and hands and how he looked at people.

I danced that opening night of *Swan Lake* at the Beijing Exhibition Hall. The performance went well. Yet I couldn't get rid of the "peasant prince" image and I was not satisfied. My aim was eventually to be as good a prince as the Western dancers, *be* that handsome prince and not just a poor peasant boy acting out a role.

Then, soon after that performance, an event occurred that would change my life forever.

Officials from the Ministry of Culture informed us that a fine choreographer and brilliant teacher, the artistic director of the Houston Ballet, was to teach two master classes at our academy. He was part of the first cultural delegation from America ever to visit communist China. The choreographer's name was Ben Stevenson.

# On the Way to the West

Twenty students, including me, were selected to attend Ben Stevenson's classes. I was exhilarated with his approach. He emphasized fluidity of movement rather than strict technique. I found him fascinating and inspiring.

After the second class, Ben offered our academy two scholarships for his annual summer school at the Houston Ballet Academy in Texas. Incredible, unbelievable news! The chance to leave China, to see the West! But Ben was told that he couldn't choose the students himself. The academy would nominate who would go.

Ben gave the invitation letter to the academy officials in March. He expected the students to be in Houston by July. Then the two students were chosen. One was a boy called Zhang Weiqiang. The other was me.

We were ecstatic. So was the whole school. It seemed too impossible to be true! How could I be going to America? *How could I?*

The academy officials thought it would be difficult for us to obtain our passports and visas so quickly, and didn't pursue the matter seriously until they received a phone call from the Ministry of Culture a few weeks later. None of them realized that Ben Stevenson had powerful friends in America. One was George H. W. Bush, who had just finished serving as the first US envoy to China after President Richard Nixon's visit in 1972. His wife, Barbara, was a trustee of the Houston Ballet. Both were well respected by the Chinese government. George Bush had formed a good relationship with Deng Xiaoping: his political connections no doubt ensured the acceptance of this scholarship invitation. Zhang Weiqiang and I were granted permission from the Ministry of Culture to go to Houston very quickly.

Our visas were approved by the American consulate in Beijing in a matter of days. We were overwhelmed with excitement. But once the euphoria faded away, panic struck. Zhang and I could speak no English. An English tutor gave us a crash course for a few days, starting with the English alphabet and ending with simple phrases such as *yes*, *no*, *good morning*, *hello*, and *good-bye*. But I really had no idea how I would make myself understood.

We went to the Ministry of Culture to be briefed by the officials. The head of the Educational Bureau, Wang Zicheng, met us briefly. He spoke with a gentle, persuasive voice. "Work hard while you're there, show your

American hosts how hard Chinese people work. Don't forget that you're representing China and the Chinese people. Treasure this opportunity. Bring back knowledge. Resist capitalist influences and make sure you exercise your communist judgment." He shook our hands and left. His assistant continued to lecture us. "Be polite at all times. If you don't understand what people are saying, just say 'yes' and smile. Never say 'no.' 'No' is a negative word. People might be offended."

She then took us into a room that contained a few racks of used Western-style suits and ties. She said they had a small supply mainly for government delegations going to foreign countries. We had never worn a suit before, only Mao jackets, but we were told to borrow one each. We tried on quite a few but they were all too big for our skinny bodies. The shoulders still came halfway down our arms and we had to fold up the sleeves. We also borrowed two ties and a suitcase each.

Zhang and I, to our utter astonishment, soon became a news item in China. We were the first official exchange artists between China and America since Chairman Mao took power in 1949.

I telephoned my parents for the first time since leaving home all those years ago. My second brother, Cunyuan, came to the commune phone first. "*Ni hao, Erga!*" I screamed excitedly.

"*Ni hao*, Cunxin! What's wrong?" he asked, sounding

191

concerned. Something dreadful must surely have happened for me to telephone.

"Nothing! I am going to America for six weeks!"

There was silence. "You're joking," he said.

"No! I'm not joking. I am going to America with another student," I replied.

"My brother is going to America!" Cunyuan screamed loudly to the people in the commune office. I could hear a roar of cheers. "I can't believe this!" he continued. "America! Niang is here . . ."

"Jing Hao!" my niang called.

"Niang, how are you?" I asked. I was so happy to hear her voice.

"I'm fine. Are you really going to America?" she asked.

"Yes, I'll be leaving in a few days."

"*Ah!* Why didn't you tell us earlier? We could have sent you some apples and dried shrimps to take on the road."

"I am going by plane. No food is allowed on the airplanes."

"On the *airplane?* How *unthinkable!* My son is going to fly on the airplane!" I heard her say to the people in the office.

"Please be careful. Stay away from the evil people in America." My niang sounded worried.

"I'm going with another student. We'll look after each other. I've also met the American dance teacher from Houston. His name is Ben. He seems nice."

"Just be careful. These foreigners are wild! They are different from us. Don't trust them."

I wasn't surprised by my niang's concerns about America. For so many years we had been told that the West, especially America, was evil. We'd heard of nothing but the mistreatment of black people, the violence on the streets, the use of firearms. Even I, who had read a few books about America since the downfall of the Gang of Four and didn't totally believe what I had learned in the past, was still suspicious and apprehensive.

⬦

Our day of departure finally arrived. That morning, eight of my friends, including the Bandit, Chong Xiongjun, and my violinist friend Liu Fengtian went out to a nearby café and brought back some pig's head meat, red sausages, pickled vegetables, watermelon, and a few jugs of warm beer. They had to smuggle the beer into the academy: we would be in trouble if we were found out by the teachers. For two hours we would enjoy our food and our companionship, before the academy's jeep took us to the airport. We speculated about what America would be like. "Don't let a big-nosed girl kidnap you over there!" said the Bandit. How he wished that he was allowed to go to the airport with me.

When it was time for Zhang and me to leave, our friends fought over carrying our luggage to the jeep and in the commotion the Bandit quietly shuffled something into my hand. "Read it on the plane," he whispered.

I quickly slipped the paper into my pocket. Before we stepped into the jeep, our friends, teachers, everyone came forward to shake our hands. Teacher Xiao was very emotional. "*Yi lu ping an!*" He wished me a safe trip and shook both my hands hard. "Cunxin! Cunxin! I know you will make China proud! Bring back new knowledge! I can't wait to share all your discoveries when you return!"

The last to say good-bye was the Bandit. Tears filled his eyes and he couldn't speak a single word. "Six weeks will disappear before you know it!" I told him.

As the jeep pulled away from our academy buildings, the last thing I saw was the Bandit's tearstained face.

I'd never been to an airport before, except the abandoned military airport near our village where I'd tried to dig up half-burned coal as a small boy. Beijing Airport was strangely quiet compared to the hustle and bustle of Beijing Station. Everything was orderly.

We were hours too early. The check-in counter wasn't even open, so Zhang Shu took us to a little canteen and bought us each a Coca-Cola. We'd heard all about Coca-Cola—the most successful invention of the Western world. I took a big mouthful and swallowed it eagerly. Too eagerly. I nearly choked with all the fizz. So did Zhang Weiqiang. We looked at each other and laughed. Our first Western experience, an American icon, and I didn't like it at all.

We said good-bye to Teacher Zhang before we checked through immigration. Zhang Weiqiang and I were now on our own. We sat in the waiting room. We hadn't a clue what to do. We looked out of the window toward the huge airplane with "China Airlines" written on it. I had never seen a plane so close. It was gigantic. How could a heavy thing like that ever get off the ground?

When the time came to board, we walked up the steps and entered the plane as a pleasant cool air seemed to cover me completely. I wondered where on earth it was coming from. I couldn't believe how big the inside of the plane was! Rows and rows of seats.

We found our own seats and waited nervously for something to happen. When it did, I nearly suffocated with excitement. As we took off I looked out of the window. My stomach churned—I didn't know whether to laugh or to scream. My heartbeat raced faster and faster, and my excitement flew higher than the clouds! Here I was, leaving behind our great nation with its steadfast beliefs forever supporting us. I felt unbelievably proud.

Our plane leveled out and once I was over the shock of the takeoff I began to explore and investigate everything I could. Movies to watch! Music to listen to! And a hostess to serve us beautiful meals: rice with fish, Japanese noodles. The hostess asked us what kind of drinks we would like. I chose something called Sprite this time.

We were treated like royalty. I felt bad just sitting there

being waited on and letting someone else do all the work. What would my niang say? So I offered to help the hostess wash the plates. She just looked at me with a very strange expression. "No, thank you," she said.

This must be a dream, I thought. Too good to be true. But when I pinched myself it hurt. I was like an ant in a hot wok. I couldn't stay still for a minute. I went through the contents of the seat pocket in front of me and found a little bag that contained unbelievable luxuries: a miniature toothbrush, toothpaste, a pair of socks, and eye covers for sleeping. Zhang and I even kept our safety cards as souvenirs. They carried a picture of the plane! What would my niang and her sewing circle think of this!

I looked around and noticed that most of the passengers on the plane seemed to be Chinese, government officials most likely. Many of them gave us rather surprised looks. Very few government officials were allowed overseas, let alone students like us.

With all the excitement of the takeoff I had forgotten about the Bandit's note. I opened the white envelope he had given me and a small piece of paper slipped out. It was a poem:

As blood brothers,
the departure of one
will never wane the love in our hearts.

Not fortune or money,
but only the pursuit of innocence and honor,
will strengthen the love in our hearts.

I thought of the past seven years and our hard and lonely life at the academy. Without the Bandit and his friendship, my life there would have been unbearable.

The three-hour flight to Tokyo went very quickly. We were told we had to get off the plane for a couple of hours at Tokyo Airport. I couldn't believe we had traveled so far in only three short hours. Zhang and I were afraid to leave the gate area in case we missed our flight. Before it was time to board, I happened to glance up at a coffee stand's price list and noticed that a cup of coffee cost US$3.00. I did a quick calculation. That was nearly half a month's salary for my dia!

This time we boarded a Northwest Airlines plane and it was even bigger than the first, a jumbo jet. It was awesome. There were endless rows of seats and we were, amazingly, ushered to an upper deck. Blankets and pillows were neatly placed on the seats and there were more gift bags and more flight safety cards for us to keep as souvenirs.

It was impossible for me to believe that I was actually sitting on this gigantic airplane on my way to the West. I looked down at the thick beautiful clouds and thought I was in the ninth heaven.

# EIGHTEEN

# "Filthy Capitalist America"

As we were about to land in Chicago, I suddenly remembered those pages from the book about the steel tycoon in Chicago, which I'd found on the street in our commune years ago, the ones that had stirred up such curiosity in my heart and mind. I longed to see if what I had learned from that book about this Paper Tiger country was true.

Zhang and I got off the plane and collected our luggage. Then we just stood there in our oversized suits. How would we recognize whoever was supposed to meet us? People around us collected their luggage, came and went, while we became more and more nervous. What if nobody showed up?

Suddenly I saw a group of people standing behind some glass windows on a second floor, and there was Ben, holding a card with my name written on it in Chinese. Zhang and I were overjoyed. Ben came to meet us just outside Immigration.

"*Ni hao*," he said, one of the few Chinese phrases he knew. "Hello," I replied, one of the few English words I knew.

I tried to use the words from my English dictionary to show Ben how ecstatic I was, but he was just happy to share our excitement with nods and smiles. When we couldn't understand his words we just smiled more and said "yes." My dictionary became my best friend from then on. Although my English was not good, Zhang's was even worse. I ended up translating for him as well.

We boarded a flight to Houston and with Ben beside us we began to relax. As we flew over the American landscape I noticed how green it was, and how it was neatly divided into squares by straight roads and streets. We saw many little square patches of blue. Ben said they were swimming pools—he mimed swimming motions with his arms. He made us laugh but I could hardly believe there could be so many swimming pools in just one area. The contrast with the bareness of China was so amazing that I started to wonder once again about America's lack of prosperity, according to the stories we'd been told.

At Houston Airport we were met by Clare Duncan, head of the Houston Ballet Academy, and two Houston Ballet board members. They handed Zhang and me a small bunch of native Texas flowers and a cowboy hat each. We didn't know whether to accept these gifts or not—we were suspicious. We simply didn't trust these Americans. I was the assigned leader of the two of us, because my political standing was higher than Zhang's, so eventually I told Zhang to accept the gifts.

The Americans' happy smiles also made us nervous. "This is not what it's supposed to be like. Something is wrong here. They are our enemies. Behind their smiling faces will be a hidden agenda. I'll find out what it is soon," I said to myself.

Like the inside of the plane, the airport was surprisingly cool. I thought we had been given the wrong information about Houston's hot weather and was thankful we had our jackets on. But the cool air didn't last long. As soon as we walked outside an intense and humid heat, like a hot wet blanket, overwhelmed us. Then one of the ballet board members, who Ben introduced as Betty Lou Bayless, ushered us into her car and it was cool in there too. Her car was so comfortable, so smooth. This was the very first time I had ever been in a car. Such luxury could only be enjoyed by government officials in China. I felt incredibly privileged.

When we passed downtown Houston and saw all the modern office buildings I thought to myself, "If Houston looks this prosperous, what would New York and Chicago be like?" Nothing I had seen so far matched the dark, decaying, depressing picture of America the Chinese government had painted in my mind. Instead I saw high-rise buildings and wide, clean streets. I knew our foreign hosts could maybe fake their behavior, but they couldn't have built these buildings just to impress us. I was confused. Someone had lied to us about America being the poorest nation in the world and China being the richest. It seemed to be the opposite. But still I was confident I would eventually find many things about America that I could hate.

We arrived at Ben's home, a large house in a fenced complex with a security gate and guards. Zhang and I were ushered inside—and my jaw dropped . . .

I saw a huge room, beautiful beyond belief, with pastel colors, sofas, and matching chairs. And giant mirrors. There was carpet—beige, soft, and bouncy. To the left I saw a kitchen—and my jaw dropped even lower. A refrigerator stood against the wall, as tall as me and four times as wide. And an electric stove and *two* sinks. The kitchen was simply enormous. Everything was new. Even the air smelled new.

Ben showed us upstairs to our bedroom, which had two single beds in it, a small walk-in closet, and the same luxurious carpet as downstairs. There were small tables with lamps beside each bed. It even had its own bathroom!

That first night in America we were taken to a local Chinese restaurant called "The Mandarin." A Chinese lady from Taiwan greeted us at the door.

The restaurant was very crowded but we were taken to our own private room. Clare Duncan and the two gentlemen we had met at the airport were there, as well as two other friends of Ben's. Zhang and I didn't know what attitude we should have toward these people. If this were China they would have been killed or jailed under Mao's regime simply because of their wealth.

We had a couple of tasty Tsingtao beers from my hometown, the first time I'd ever had one, and as the evening progressed we gradually let our guard down a little and joined in the fun. Ben ordered many delicious dishes, including Peking Duck. I'd never had Peking Duck before either, and it just melted in my mouth. "No one is going to believe me back home," I thought.

Many courses later, Ben asked us if we were still hungry. We didn't understand what he was saying, but we remembered that we had to keep smiling and saying, "Yes, yes!" just as the Chinese officials had told us. More and more food kept arriving. Eventually I just held my head and shouted, "Oh dear me!" and everyone burst into roars of laughter.

In desperation I went to the Chinese lady who owned the restaurant. "Can you please tell Ben to stop ordering any more food? Our stomachs will simply burst!"

"But he hasn't even ordered dessert yet," she said.

I'd never heard of dessert.

By the end of the evening we had so much leftover food on the table I asked Ben if we could take it home. I couldn't bear the waste. I thought of all the starvation in China. Everyone that night seemed to admire our slimness and I couldn't understand why. In China being thin was a symbol of poverty; being fat meant you had money to buy good food. Later I discovered that many people in America went to expensive diet clinics to lose weight. I could easily help them, I thought, just by sending them to China and feeding them dried yams for a while.

When we got back to Ben's place I had my first bath. The water soaked my body and soothed my every nerve. The bed was a different matter though. I found the soft bouncy mattress very uncomfortable!

When I woke up the next morning I had to pinch myself to make sure that everything was real. When I heard Ben's voice downstairs calling us for breakfast, I knew it was true. I *was* in America. For six whole weeks.

Ben had already cooked us some bacon and eggs. "Would you like some muffins?" he asked.

Zhang and I exchanged horrified looks. "No, thank you!" we replied quickly. "What a terrible thing for Ben to offer us for breakfast," I thought to myself.

This time Ben was puzzled. "What's wrong?"

With the help of my dictionary, I replied: "'Muffin' meaning horse poop in Chinese."

Ben roared with laughter. "First 'Oh dear me' and now 'horse poop!' We're going to have a lot of fun this summer."

Next he offered us orange juice. I felt like a criminal drinking that precious juice. My family had never even seen an orange before. And it was the first time that we'd ever tasted bacon, toast, butter, and jam. We had *masses* of food. Ben couldn't believe where it all went. He had to cook more bacon and fry more eggs. It was as though we hadn't eaten for eighteen years.

The Houston Ballet Academy was in a single-story brick building shared with the Houston Ballet Company. There were four medium-sized studios.

Clare Duncan, the head of the academy, took us around and introduced us to the teachers and students. Zhang and I were completely confused. Everyone looked alike and their names were impossible to remember.

"Ballet class, when?" I asked Ben, with the aid of my dictionary. I was eager to begin.

"You can start today if you like," he replied.

When I looked into the studios I noticed all the male students wore black tights, white T-shirts, socks, and shoes. The only pair of tights I had was given to me by one of my teachers back in China. He'd gotten them from a British ballet dancer and they were bright blue.

"No pants," I told Ben after I found the word "pants" in my dictionary.

"You don't need pants for class." Ben was puzzled.

"Pants, pants!" I repeated as I demonstrated a plié and pointed at my legs.

"You don't need pants, you only need . . . oh, *tights!* "

"Yes!" I wasn't sure what the word "tights" meant but it looked like Ben had understood, so I smiled broadly.

He quickly organized for us to go to a dancewear shop. He gave Stephanie, the company manager, enough money to buy Zhang and me two pairs of tights, dance belts, and a pair of ballet shoes, which cost over $200 each. I quickly did a currency conversion: $200 was equivalent to over two years of my dia's salary. How could I justify Ben spending two years' salary on our dancewear!

It was lunchtime when we arrived back at the academy and a Houston Ballet board member, Louisa Sarofim, was waiting to take us to lunch at a nearby restaurant.

From the way the restaurant owner treated Louisa, I knew we were about to have lunch with yet another class enemy. The restaurant was amazingly elegant and cool.

We were handed a menu each. I couldn't read anything except the prices. Since Louisa was going to pay, I thought I should be modest and not order anything too expensive. I didn't want to leave a bad impression. I told Zhang of my intentions. "I will do the same," he said. We chose two of the cheapest items on the menu. I hadn't any idea what I'd ordered but was confident that we wouldn't be left starving.

Minutes later, the waiter placed a small plate of green salad in front of me and a small bowl of green soup in front of Zhang. I still remember the look Zhang gave me. I forced out a smile and quickly turned my eyes away.

"Are you okay?" Ben asked, concerned.

"Okay!" I replied brightly. I poked my fork into the greens and tasted a leaf of my very first salad. "Good taste!" I said to Zhang, to encourage him. He forced himself to finish his green soup. Luckily the waiter kept circling our table with freshly baked bread.

Louisa dropped us back at the studio, which was packed with dancers when we arrived. On the center barre the students moved up to make room for Zhang and me. Then Ben walked in. His energy and his passion for teaching seemed to inspire everybody. During the class I kept a keen eye on other students and to my surprise I discovered Zhang and I compared well. The precision of our technique was high; this could only have come about from the strict discipline of our Chinese training.

There were students here from England, Canada, and other places, a result of Ben's international reputation as a teacher, choreographer, and artistic director. Our schedule was full each day. There were many classes— ballet, character, modern ballet, pas de deux, body conditioning, and choreographic workshops. I wasn't sure what to expect in the modern ballet class, but our Chinese folk dance classes and tai chi movements made it easy for us to find some common ground. The body conditioning class was different—it was based on something called Pilates, and I could see it would help me understand my own body and deal with my weaknesses and injuries.

In Houston we were even given fifty dollars per week as a living allowance. I never dreamed of having that amount of money in my entire life! Eight months of my dia's wages! I tried to save as much money as possible so I could help my family when I returned to China.

❧

We soon discovered that Ben was a very good cook and loved entertaining, so we were surrounded by people all the time we were there. That meant a lot of nodding and smiling on our part.

During that second week in Houston, Ben's good friend Barbara Bush invited us to her house for lunch. I remember she even had an indoor pool. She apologized for her husband's absence: he had to attend a presidential rally in California that day.

I felt very privileged to meet Barbara, but her husband was such a high-profile politician that I was deeply suspicious of her hidden political agenda. Would she try to corrupt our political beliefs? But all we received was generosity and friendliness. Barbara reminded me of my niang. She talked about China very fondly.

That day we'd been asked to bring our swimming suits. We didn't have any, so Ben had to buy them for us, like so many other things. Barbara and Ben chatted happily while Zhang and I swam in a pool owned by one of the most powerful ladies in America.

Barbara had a little dog called Fred. She adored Fred.

She'd even taken him to China while Mr. Bush served as the first envoy. She told us that Fred was very intelligent. I thought that if her dog had been in my hometown, someone would have eaten him for dinner.

We went to board member Louisa Sarofim's house a few times too. I couldn't believe her wealth. I saw some of the most beautiful paintings I had ever seen. Ben told me later that they were worth millions of dollars. A million dollars? She had so much money, yet she was so nice and unpretentious and she loved ballet and took immense pride in the Houston Ballet. The amount of wealth surrounding ballet in America seemed amazing. Sometimes I heard people talking of hundreds of millions of dollars. Such numbers didn't exist in my vocabulary. The financial and cultural gaps were simply too great to comprehend.

During the first week of the summer school, Ben arranged for us to attend an English language course and I began to learn ten to fifteen new words a day. I carried a piece of paper everywhere I went, with my new English words written on it. The most effective place for me to learn them was in the bathroom. My English improved quickly, and I went on translating for Zhang.

I was constantly surprised by how much freedom the American people had. One day in the academy one of the students from New Orleans noticed my Mao button on my dance bag.

"Do you like your Chairman Mao?" he asked.

"I love Chairman Mao!" I replied with my fist over my heart.

"Well, I don't like our president Jimmy Carter. I don't think he's a good president at all," he said and pointed his thumb down.

"Shh . . . !" I looked around nervously. "You not scared people listen to you talk about your big leader this way?"

"I can say anything I like about our president. This is America."

"If I say bad thing about Chairman Mao," I whispered, "I will go jail and may be killed."

"You're kidding!"

"Is true!" I replied.

Ben choreographed a dance for Zhang and me over the next few weeks using George Gershwin's music. We had difficulties understanding what Ben wanted us to do in the rehearsals because of our minimal understanding of English. Also, although Zhang and I could easily complete the difficult and challenging turns and jumps, taking an effortless walk across the studio without turning out our feet or pointing our toes was a real challenge. At one point Ben grabbed my arms and shook my entire body. "Relax, relax!" he shouted. Then he rushed over to Zhang and did the same. When I finally got the hang of what Ben wanted, it felt like cheating. It was too easy and casual. It didn't feel like dancing at all. But I *could* sense the gradual progression and developments in Gershwin's music and Ben's choreography meshing into it.

By the end of our six-week stay I had started to relax. I began to make friends among the students, the dancers in the company, and even some board members. Each weekend we had to report to the Chinese consulate. One of the senior consuls was Zhang Zongshu, whose wife was a translator. They were assigned to look after us.

It turned out that Ben had decided to ask Consul Zhang if I could come back to work with the company again. Consul Zhang and the Chinese consulate sent a favorable report to the Ministry of Culture. I was granted permission to return for a *whole year* to work with the Houston Ballet, only two months after my scheduled return to China. There were also discussions about the possibility of Zhang Weiqiang's return.

The thought of being able to come back to America made me happy. I was so grateful to the Chinese government. I felt that they really cared for me. For me, a peasant boy. Communism truly was great.

For our last few days in America, Ben took Zhang and me to Washington DC and New York. We didn't do much in Washington except pose for photos in front of the White House and the Kennedy Center. In some ways I was disappointed. I had expected to see a massive number of security guards with machine guns, just like those I'd seen in Beijing. But there were only a few guards standing by a small gate, looking rather relaxed. They even let us stand next to the fence to have our pictures taken.

Ben rushed Zhang and me around like mad to see as many of the great sites of New York as possible—the Twin Towers, the Empire State Building, the Statue of Liberty, Central Park . . . I was in awe of this hustling, bustling city. Everything surprised and impressed me— the gigantic buildings, the number of cars, the cleanliness compared to Beijing. Then a friend of Ben's showed us a thing called an ATM. I was speechless when twenty-dollar bills began spewing out. To see money coming out of a wall was beyond my wildest imaginings. I couldn't stop comparing everything to China and my family's life back home.

We returned to Houston for our last two days before heading back to China. People gave us farewell gifts. Ben had made our stay such a positive experience and was proud to have arranged for the first two Chinese cultural exchange students to come to America. He'd been thoughtful and generous, protective and kind. He had poured special interest into our dancing. I knew I could never repay him. When Zhang and I said our final good-bye to Ben at the airport, we felt sad to be leaving a special friend.

On the plane I thought of the possibility of returning to Houston in only two months' time. I thought of how I'd felt about America and its people before I came. I laughed when I remembered my initial suspicions.

Most of all I thought of those dark, scary images of capitalist society and how they had now been replaced by an entirely different picture in my mind. China's most hated enemy and the system it represented had given me something that was my heart's desire. Now I was frightened and confused. What should I believe? What communism had taught me? Or what I'd seen and experienced? Why had Chairman Mao, Madame Mao, and the Chinese government told its people all those lies about America? Why were we so poor in China? Why was America so prosperous?

I kept resisting my doubts all the way home on the plane back to China. I tried to tell myself that my strong communist faith was still unshakeable, but I knew I was lying to myself. I knew I had to believe what the Chinese government wanted me to believe, or at least to pretend to. All this made me even more afraid. I was never supposed to question my communist beliefs. I never, ever thought that I would. So I kept telling myself that I was happy to return to China, because that's where my family, friends, and teachers were.

But still the doubts persisted. I had tasted freedom, and I couldn't lie to myself about that.

# Good-bye, China

The first thing I did when I returned to the Beijing Dance Academy was to tell Teacher Xiao, Zhang Shu, the Bandit, and all my friends about my new discoveries in dance: the Gershwin pas de deux, the Martha Graham technique, the body conditioning classes. I couldn't hide my excitement and enthusiasm. I had decided, however, that I wouldn't say anything about how much I liked America. I especially wouldn't mention the sense of freedom I had experienced. I knew it would give the authorities reason to deny me permission to return to America. As an old Chinese saying goes, "The wind will carry the words to other people's ears."

That freedom occupied my mind constantly. In China, Chairman Mao and his government's absolute authority could never have been challenged. We didn't have individual rights. We were told what to do, how long to work each day, how much we would be paid, where we would live, how many children we were allowed to have. I struggled with my communist beliefs: memories of America were so fresh. What if *I* were to have that same freedom? What could I do with my ballet then?

I talked myself into believing that if I had stayed in America any longer I would surely have seen so many bad things about capitalism that I wouldn't have liked America at all. Even so, I was surprised that I was wavering after spending only six weeks there. How could eighteen years of communism be so easily influenced by six short weeks of capitalism? Without Chairman Mao I was lost. Would I still die for him? I wasn't sure anymore.

I also started to question aspects of our ballet training in China. I couldn't wait for the two months to pass so I could go back to America and continue my learning.

Zhang and I had to report to Director Song of our academy and to the Ministry of Culture, which required a written report from us about our American trip.

"Would you like to meet this evening to work on the report with me?" I asked Zhang.

"Why don't you just write it yourself," replied Zhang. "I trust you."

I was happy that Zhang trusted me to complete this task but I found it very difficult to write bad things about America. I made up some bad things about "rotten capitalist influences." First I described the daily routine at the Houston Ballet Academy and the new experiences in Ben's ballet classes. I emphasized the goodwill Zhang and I had generated for China. Then I put a considerable amount of effort into describing the diseased aspects of America. I described the restaurant owner from Taiwan as one of our class enemies and a black neighborhood in Houston with its decaying houses. I expressed sorrow for the poor black people. I emphasized our superior communist system and Chairman Mao's principles.

"This is great! Thank you, Cunxin!" Zhang said enthusiastically after he'd read the report.

But I felt angry that I'd had to do this at all.

When we handed in our report and returned the borrowed suitcases, ties, and suits to the ministry, Wang Zicheng's deputy also asked us to relinquish any living allowance we'd been given.

Zhang and I were shocked. "We spent most of the money on food while we were there," I replied.

"I want every remaining dollar here by tomorrow," she demanded.

Being good and honest Red Guards we gave all our remaining money to the ministry the following day. I was desperately disappointed—my family needed it more than the ministry did.

Going back to America so soon meant that I wouldn't be able to see my parents until after my return the following year. I knew they'd be eager to hear from me, so I wrote them a letter. *I will miss you dreadfully*, I wrote, *especially on New Year's Eve. I will raise my glass full of Tsingtao beer in a*

*faraway foreign land and drink to your health and happiness. I will*
*kneel and kowtow to you. If you sneeze, you will know that it is prob-*
*ably because I am mentioning your names. I hope you will understand*
*how much I want to come home and tell you everything about Amer-*
*ica. It would take me too long to write it all down. Please be patient*
*and wait for another year. Before you know it I'll be back. I have*
*brought presents back for you. I will bring them home next year. I am*
*sending with this letter a flight safety card so you can see the picture*
*of the plane I flew on. I wish you could have the chance to fly one*
*day. I'm sending with this letter all the love in my heart. I want to tell*
*Niang that I miss her dumplings and all her delicious food.*

On the third day after I returned, Zhang Shu asked me to
teach a master class to all the ballet teachers in the academy
to show them what I had learned while I was away. Teach
my teachers? I felt nervous about that, but it went well.

I was happy to see my good friends at the Beijing Dance
Academy again, especially the Bandit. I gave him an "I Love
New York" button and some postcards from the cities I'd
been to. He wasn't sure he'd be able to wear the button in
public, but he loved it all the same.

"You didn't fall in love with a pretty big-nosed girl
while you were there?" he asked suddenly.

I laughed. "Don't be silly. Of course not!"

"What do you *really* think about America?" he asked.

I hesitated. I wasn't sure what to say. I wanted to tell him
about the freedom I had tasted but I knew this would make
him miserable. "There were many clean and wide streets,

a lot of cars, tall buildings, and good living standards," I said instead. "But the best thing was Ben. He was so kind and I love his teaching." Then I told him about the White House, about New York, and all the electronic gadgets. He was especially excited about the ATM machine. I told him I hoped he'd have the chance to see it all for himself one day, and quickly changed the subject.

I received my visa papers from Houston toward the end of the second week and immediately went to the Ministry of Culture to reapply for my passport. But when I arrived the deputy had some devastating news. "Cunxin," she said casually, "I've just received a directive from the minister's office. The minister has changed his mind. He has refused your request for a passport."

I couldn't believe what I was hearing.

"The minister is concerned about potential Western influences. He thinks you are too young."

"But I've been there once already and the Western influence did nothing to me! Didn't you read our report?"

"Yes, I did. But the minister has made up his mind."

I walked out of the building in total despair.

Back at our academy I charged into Director Song's office. "Director Song, did you know about this?"

"Yes, but only this morning. The minister thinks you are too young to go to America by yourself. It is a dark and filthy world out there."

"But the minister already gave me permission before I left America!" I said, full of emotion. "I have to go back! To learn more, to serve our country better!"

"I understand your feelings. But you must trust the decision of the party. You shouldn't question the wisdom of the minister's decision. You are only a tiny part of the communist cause. Forget your personal desires."

I left Director Song's office frustrated and angry. I walked right out of the academy. By this time they were more relaxed about senior students coming and going, so the security guard didn't stop me. I needed time to think, so I went to Taoranting Park. I walked faster and faster. I began to run without any thought or purpose, trying to drive away what was in my mind and heart. It was as though a beautiful sunny day, without warning, had turned dark and unfamiliar. All I could see was a never-ending road leading nowhere. My heart was racing, my legs were cramping, and I gasped for air. "I have to get out!" I kept telling myself.

Seeing the willows swaying from side to side in the breeze, I longed for refuge once again. I climbed onto a small tree and spoke to the weeping willows for the first time in five and a half years. How could my opportunity to go back to America be taken away just like that?

America was real. I had seen it. The plane trips, the cars, the cowboy hats, the steaks, the raw salad, the ballet classes, the Gershwin music. It was all so vivid and close.

Desperately I tried to think of the real reason why the minister had changed his mind. Was it my report? Did I write too many good things about America? Or was what I'd been told by the deputy true?

I had no answers, but I would do everything I could to find out the truth. "Calm down, Cunxin," I told myself. "Think of ways to persuade the minister to change his mind."

I went back to the academy. "Teacher Xiao is looking for you!" the Bandit shouted from a distance as soon as he spotted me. "Are you all right? You look terrible."

"I'm not allowed to go back to America," I replied.

"Why?" cried the Bandit.

I couldn't say. Tears choked my throat. I ran to Teacher Xiao's office and knocked on the door.

As soon as I closed the door he rushed up to me and hugged me tight. "I heard the news. I'm sorry," he whispered.

I was stunned by his hug at first. Hugging still wasn't a communist thing to do. "Why, *why* did he take it away from me?" I sobbed. "What did I do wrong?"

"Sit down," Teacher Xiao said. He pulled a chair out from under his small desk and lit a cigarette. "According to Director Song, the minister feels that you are too young to go to the West for a whole year."

"But he gave me permission to go back before I returned! What made him change his mind?"

"I don't know. Teacher Zhang and I asked the same question."

"Is there any way we can find out?" I persisted.

"You never give up, do you?" Teacher Xiao smiled. "Teacher Zhang and I have convinced Director Song to send a petition to Minister Wang to see if he will change his mind. Now all we can do is wait."

"Thank you, Teacher Xiao," I said.

"Don't thank me. You need to thank Teacher Zhang. He did most of the talking. We both felt that after only six weeks in America your dancing had already improved enormously. I can't imagine what a year would do for you. Ben Stevenson can give you opportunities we cannot offer here. Now, go to dinner," he urged. "Otherwise there will be nothing left."

I didn't hear back from the ministry for over a week. Then, on a Tuesday, Zhang Shu called me into his office. Teacher Xiao was already there. As soon as I entered the room I sensed the news was bad.

"Cunxin," Zhang Shu said, "our petition has been turned down. I'm so sorry."

I tried hard to hold back my tears.

Teacher Xiao said, "Teacher Zhang and I have decided to give you permission to take three weeks holiday to visit your family. You haven't seen them for nearly two years. I'm sure they are missing you."

"Thank you," I said, and stumbled out of the office.

A door to a whole new world had shut right in front of me. I was devastated. Just as I'd done on that very first night at the Beijing Dance Academy seven years ago, I plunged onto my bed and under my niang's quilt.

I couldn't understand why not going back to America was affecting me so much. I became angry with myself for being so selfish. I was lucky to go to America once and I should be satisfied and thankful. Yet a stronger voice kept rising above all other voices in my mind: "I want to go back. I want to study with Ben. I want to improve my dancing—and most importantly I want to taste that precious freedom once again."

I jumped out of bed and ran to Teacher Xiao's office. "Teacher Xiao, do you know where Minister Wang lives?"

He frowned. "Yes, why?"

"I want to see him."

"I don't think he will see you even if you do go to his residence. I think you would be better to go to the ministry and make an appointment with his assistant instead."

"I don't think his office will let me make an appointment. He has already refused my case twice. Besides, he is not a tiger. He won't eat me, will he?" I was remembering what Teacher Xiao had said to me once about Teacher Gao.

"You and your memory," he said. "I will never underestimate either your memory or your resolve." He wrote the minister's address on a small piece of paper and handed it to me. "Good luck," he said.

The following evening I took two different buses to Minister Wang's residence. It was an impressive compound with high walls and a tall, metal-barred security gate. There was a guardhouse and a military guard with a machine gun at the ready.

"Hello, Comrade," I said to the guard as confidently as I could. "I'm Li Cunxin from the Beijing Dance Academy. I'm here to see Minister Wang."

"Do you have an appointment?" he asked.

"No, I don't," I replied honestly.

"Go home if you don't have an appointment," the guard growled.

"I only need to see him for one minute. Please, it's an urgent matter," I begged.

"Go home. You cannot see the minister without an appointment. Move! Or I'll have you arrested."

I left, angry and humiliated. This was not how comrades should treat each other.

I was back the following night. This time, a different guard was at the gate.

"Hello, Comrade. I'm Li Cunxin from the Beijing Dance Academy, and I've just returned from America representing China. I was told to meet Minister Wang tonight," I lied.

"What time is your appointment?" he asked.

"I'm not sure. Our academy made the appointment."

"Wait a minute. What did you say your name was?"

"Li," I replied, hoping he wouldn't ask for my first name. Li is a very common family name in China. I prayed that someone else called Li had an appointment with the minister that night.

"I don't see any appointments made with the minister tonight," the guard said, checking the appointment book. "Are you sure you've come on the right date? The minister is attending a banquet. He won't be back until late."

"I'm sorry, I must have the date wrong. Thank you." I walked to the end of the street, turned the corner, then sat on a stone doorstep and waited for the minister's return. I went over what I was going to say to him, keeping an eye out for his car.

By midnight I was freezing and tired and there was still no sign of the minister. I ran to the nearby bus stop to shake off the cold and caught the last bus back. At the academy the security guard was already asleep and I climbed over the gate as quietly as a cat.

The next day after our ballet class Teacher Xiao called me to his office. "I'm worried about you. Why don't you give yourself a break?" he said.

I shook my head and told him what I'd done the last two nights. "I won't give up until every possible avenue has been explored," I said defiantly.

"Cunxin, for all the years I've known you, I have never once doubted your determination. But here you are dealing with things beyond your control. Like a flea trying to overpower an elephant."

"Isn't there any other way?"

Teacher Xiao shook his head. "The minister rarely reverses his decisions."

But still I would not give up. On the third night I returned to Minister Wang's residence. This time I wore more clothes and was prepared to wait all night.

The same guard from the first night greeted me. "Hello, Comrade. Do you have an appointment this time?"

"Yes, one of my teachers has made an appointment with the minister's deputy and I was to meet him tonight at seven thirty," I said matter-of-factly.

"Wait here."

My heart thumped. I hated myself for lying.

A few minutes later, the guard came back. "You can't even lie properly! Go home and don't come back until you have a proper appointment."

In spite of his words, I noticed he was in a better mood than the first night. "Comrade, I'm sorry that I have to lie to you but I *must* see Minister Wang, even just for one minute." I told him the reason I wanted to see the minister. I begged him to give me a chance. "I promise I'll only take one minute of his time."

"Okay, but I don't know when the minister will be back, and I can't guarantee that he will see you."

This time I didn't have to hide at the end of the street. I

walked back and forth, going over what I would say to the minister for the hundredth time.

Just before ten o'clock the guard called me over. "I am going inside at midnight. If the minister is still not back I can't guarantee my replacement will let you hang around." Then he hesitated. "What's America like?" he asked.

"What do you want to know?" I asked.

"Anything!" he replied eagerly.

I told him about the cars, the tall buildings, the ATM machines . . .

"People can get money out of a machine in a wall?" He was very amused.

I was careful not to show too much enthusiasm about America. When I told him about the guards at the White House with no machine guns, he was amazed.

"It's true. Security is very lax there."

"Is the White House really white?" he asked.

"Yes," I replied, trying to sound as though I didn't care much about the White House at all.

"I can't believe they let a Chinese ballet student get so close!" Under the dim light I could see his expression of disbelief. To leave no doubt in his mind about my commitment to communism, I told him that I despised our class enemies in America and I was sympathetic toward the American poor. But I could tell he was more interested in hearing about things like ATM machines.

About an hour later, two bright headlights appeared from one end of the street.

"Stand aside, this is him," the guard said and quickly walked to the driver's side. I couldn't hear what he said but a couple of minutes later the minister's car drove through the entrance. The guard pulled the gate closed. "Sorry, Xiao Li. The minister didn't want to see you."

"What did you tell him?" My heart was still palpitating.

"I told him why you were here and that you'd been here for several nights. But all he said was 'Drive on.' He was rather annoyed."

I walked away under the faint streetlight. That was my very last chance. I would never go back to America now. I had been beaten. "How could you think your existence would mean so much to the communist cause!" I told myself. "Do you imagine an important leader such as Minister Wang would spend a single second thinking about you, a mere peasant boy?" How foolish to believe everyone was equal in China. I had believed this communist doctrine for so many years. But in the minister's eyes I was no one. He didn't even bother to glance out of his car at this eager and pathetic boy.

I thought bitterly of the minister riding away in his flashy car. I thought of a story we'd been told at school about Mao not eating pork, deliberately suffering hardships just like the rest of us, and I seethed with rage.

I realized then that China was like any other nation on

earth. There was no equality. But I, like all the Chinese people, had given Chairman Mao and his government my unwavering support for so many years. I never questioned them. What choice did we have? "Cunxin, it's time to wake up. The government and Minister Wang are no longer there for you. You have to look after yourself. You only have one life to live," I told myself.

I went back to the academy and lay awake until the early hours of the morning.

I didn't hear the wake-up bell. I didn't wake when the Bandit shook me at lunchtime, and I slept through the morning classes and afternoon rehearsals. I felt someone putting his hand on my forehead to feel my temperature. "Cunxin has a fever," I heard them say. My throat throbbed. My bones ached. My entire body was burning. But the most painful thing was my memory of the night before. Sleep was the only thing that would cure my misery and shaken beliefs. I held on to my niang's quilt for dear life.

Finally I heard the voices of Teacher Xiao and the Bandit. "Wake up, Cunxin, wake up!"

I forced myself to open my eyes and look at their kind, caring faces. "Leave me alone. I want to go back to my dreams."

"Cunxin, listen to me!" Teacher Xiao said. "You have two choices. Think of this as a card game: you can simply give up and stop participating or you can play on and see what happens. You have a long life and career in front of you. There will be triumphs as well as setbacks, but if you give up now you will never succeed!"

I looked first at Teacher Xiao and then at the Bandit. I burst into uncontrollable sobs. My anger, my disappointment, my injured pride and shattered beliefs all forced their way out.

The next day, from Director Song's office, I made a phone call to Ben Stevenson in Houston. "I cannot come," I told him. "My big leader in government say no."

He asked me some questions I didn't really understand. The only words I detected were "why," "disappointed," and "sad." I kept asking him to repeat. Eventually he screamed down the phone in sheer frustration: "You! Come! Later!"

"No. Big leader say no. I. Write. Letter. For you."

After I had spoken to Ben, I immediately phoned my village and asked for my parents. "Fifth Brother, it's Cunxin. I am coming home."

"Aren't you going back to America?" he asked, surprised.

"No, not anymore," I replied.

"Why? What's wrong?"

"Nothing is wrong. I will explain when I get back. The Minister of Culture thinks I'm too young to go back alone. I will call you once I get my train ticket." I quickly put the phone down.

Two days later I purchased my train ticket, ready to go home for a three-week holiday. But that afternoon, as I was scanning through the *People's Daily* newspaper, a headline caught my eye: MINISTER WANG, THE MINISTER OF CULTURE, WILL LEAD A DELEGATION TO SOUTH AMERICA FOR FIVE WEEKS.

I pulled the paper to my chest as though I had found a treasure and immediately ran to Teacher Xiao's office.

"Teacher Xiao, Teacher Xiao! Read this!"

"I've read it already. The minister is going to South America for five weeks. What's strange about that?"

"Who will be in charge of the ministry while he's gone?" I asked.

Teacher Xiao suddenly understood. We walked down to level two together and knocked on Zhang Shu's door.

"There may be a way for Cunxin to go to America after all," Teacher Xiao said.

Teacher Xiao handed Zhang Shu the newspaper. He quickly scanned the headline.

"We can lobby the vice-minister in charge to ask permission for Cunxin to leave!" Teacher Xiao shouted excitedly.

"The vice-minister might be reluctant to take on the responsibility knowing Minister Wang refused it before," Zhang Shu said thoughtfully.

"Can't we lobby *all* the vice-ministers?" I suggested.

They looked at each other and laughed. "All five of them?" Zhang Shu shook his head.

They then discussed who was the key vice-minister and decided on Lin Muhan, a well-known intellect in China, a labeled rightist who had been through some horrifying times during the Cultural Revolution. He was now in charge of the educational area within the ministry and a strong advocate for talent. Zhang Shu felt he would be sympathetic toward my situation.

I wrote to my family and told them that I couldn't go home just yet.

Our intense lobbying lasted over two weeks. Years later, Teacher Xiao told me that he and Zhang Shu had even gone to Lin Muhan's residence in their final effort to get me back to America. This time they succeeded. Lin Muhan lobbied the four other vice-ministers and signed the permission for me to go to America for one year.

Passport in hand, I went to the US consulate in Beijing and my visa was granted within days.

I telephoned Ben. "I can come! Plane ticket, please!" I shouted, my heart blossoming like a flower.

My reservation was confirmed. I was to leave China in three days.

My last three days were frantically busy. All my friends wanted some special time alone with me. On Saturday night, Teacher Xiao invited the entire class to his apartment and cooked us a delicious meal. We all helped. We banged our glasses together and shouted, "*Gan bei!*"

Teacher Xiao stood up and raised his glass. "I wish to propose two toasts. The first is to all of you for putting up with me for over five and a half years of shouting and carrying on. This may be our last gathering together. I'm proud to be your teacher and I wish you all the best of luck. You're Chairman and Madame Mao's last generation of dancers. You have studied under the most strict and disciplined rules imaginable, but this will give you an edge over the others." Teacher Xiao stopped briefly to calm his emotions. "I'll boldly make a prediction. Your dancing will proudly stand high in Chinese ballet history."

He paused again. "My second toast is to Cunxin's American trip." He looked at me. "I hope you will respect your past and charge toward the future. Perfect your art form. Make all of China proud. *Gan bei!*"

This was the very last time our class would ever gather together with Teacher Xiao.

I felt so happy about going back to America but I wished that I could go home to my family before I went. I longed to see my parents and brothers, but I couldn't take the risk of going to Qingdao. The possibility of the ministers changing their minds was very real. I had to be content with seeing my family in a year's time.

I visited my adopted family, the Chongs, that Sunday,

and afterward at the Beijing Dance Academy, the Bandit, Liu Fengtian, Chong Xiongjun, and some of my classmates organized a farewell party. The mood was happy and warm, but there was also a sense of sadness—no one knew if we would ever gather together like this again.

In November 1979, a month after my original planned date, I left China for the second time.

# PART THREE

## The West

# TWENTY

# Return to the Land of Freedom

The plane soared into the air. The past few months had worn me out and up to the last seconds before takeoff I feared that the Chinese government might still change its mind and I would be dragged off the plane.

I so desperately wanted a freedom of expression and thought that I couldn't have in China, and to conquer the ballet world. And here was my chance. Now I wouldn't have to dance for Mao's communist ideals. Now I could dance for myself, my parents, my teachers, and my friends back in China. The communist influence was fading fast.

Janie Parker, one of the principal dancers of the Houston Ballet, picked me up from Houston Airport. She drove me back to Ben's place through perfect autumn weather. I thought of the filthy, dusty Beijing air and opened the car window to let the fresh, clean Houston air gust against my face. I took a deep breath. My spirit felt free.

I was to stay for twelve months. My beliefs were now completely altered after my experience with the Ministry of Culture and after having the time to think about what I'd seen in the West. I realized that I had been manipulated by Chairman Mao's communist propaganda for many years.

⚬

During my first month back at the Houston Ballet Academy I kept discovering and experimenting with new things. I carried my list of new English words with me everywhere. There were classes and rehearsals during the day and keeping up with Ben's busy social schedule in the evenings. I tried to record something in my diary at least every other day, first in Chinese—then, as I increased my English vocabulary, my diary became 50 percent Chinese, 30 percent English, and the rest was French ballet terminology.

Ben started rehearsals for *Nutcracker* soon after I arrived. Ben's *Nutcracker* was completely different from the Baryshnikov version, but I immediately fell in love with it. It had the freedom of expression I'd been longing for. I had two solo roles in my first ballet with the company.

It was through *Nutcracker* that I first noticed Lori Langlinais. She was in her early twenties, a talented dancer, full of life. Her contagious laugh reminded me of my niang's. We quickly became good friends, she treating me like a little brother while I regarded her as a big sister. We used to call each other "Big Ballerina" and "Big Ballerino."

I made many new friends. With Christmas approaching, one of Ben's friends bought me a book about Christmas. With the help of my dictionary and the pictures, I worked out that on Christmas Eve this long-silver-bearded man called Santa Claus would ride on a sled pulled by nine reindeer, all with very strange names. I remembered the one called Rudolph, because of Rudolf Nureyev. What was even stranger was that Santa Claus went down people's chimneys and put presents in children's stockings!

Most of what I learned about Christmas, however, was to do with shopping. With my limited scholarship money I bought a few presents for my American friends when Ben took me to a famous shopping mall. There was a mass of people there, everyone carrying enormous numbers of bags. Christmas trees were everywhere. Ben spent nearly $5,000 on presents in a couple of hours. My father's salary for sixty-five years! My father's entire lifetime of backbreaking work. My family could live on this amount for over half a century. It was shocking.

The Christmas Day party at Ben's house was a megaevent, with over forty friends, dancers, and students. Ben had presents for everyone. I even received presents from Santa Claus, left in my very own Christmas stocking hanging in Ben's living room. Ben didn't have a fireplace: I wondered how Santa had got in.

Ben's Christmas food was a feast. A huge sizzling turkey, a big shining ham, trays of roasted potatoes, cakes, and puddings. I kept telling myself to enjoy it, but all I could think of was dried yams and my family's survival.

⚶

The months passed quickly. That summer my friend Zhang Weiqiang received permission from the Ministry of Culture to come back for summer school, along with three more students from the Beijing Dance Academy. I was so happy to see them and thrilled they also had the opportunity to come to the West.

During the summer session I met an eighteen-year-old girl from Florida called Elizabeth Mackey. She sat right next to me during floor exercises. I felt self-conscious sitting so close. She wore her long hair loose and I noticed the subtle smell of her perfume.

Throughout the summer school Elizabeth and I kept bumping into each other. Whenever our eyes met my heart beat faster. But I kept telling myself, "Don't be silly. Remember the Bandit's unrequited love? Concentrate on your dancing. You are not worthy of such a beautiful girl."

I had other things to concentrate on. Ben called me one day. "Li, Billy has just injured his back. Would you like to replace him and dance with Suzanne Longley tonight?"

My heart leaped. Suzanne and Billy were principal dancers in the company. He and Suzanne were guest artists that night, dancing Ben's pas de deux in the Houston Grand Opera's *Die Fledermaus* in an outdoor theater.

"But I don't know steps!" I shouted into the phone.

"I'll teach you. Hurry up, we'll wait for you."

I ran all the way to the studio. It took me just over three hours to learn every step of the grand pas de deux. We barely had time to eat before going to the theater for our stage rehearsal at 6:30 p.m. I had never been so nervous in my life. I wasn't just nervous. I was petrified. What if I forgot the choreography? What if the audience booed? "Cunxin, just remember to breathe and let the music help you. And whatever you do, don't let Suzanne fall to the ground," I told myself.

As the introduction music for our pas de deux was played, Suzanne looked at me with a radiant smile. I forced a smile back. "This is it," I thought. "The test of your seven years training under Madame Mao. Remember your parents. Remember Teacher Xiao. Remember the Bandit and the Chinese people."

Suzanne and I charged onto the stage. My calves didn't cramp. I didn't forget any choreography. I was too nervous to know how well I danced but Suzanne gave me the biggest hug after the performance.

Ben read me the reviews the next day: America had discovered a new star, from China of all places, they said.

After my success with Suzanne, there seemed to be a magnet drawing me back to the academy. Hardly anyone was there because it was a holiday. Then, to my great surprise, I saw Elizabeth practicing alone in a small studio.

"Hello." She smiled. With my heart racing I timidly entered the studio. "I thought you had gone away with Ben," she said.

"I did," I told her, "but now I am back."

"Would you like me to take you anywhere?" she asked. "I have a car."

"No, thank you," I replied politely. Then suddenly I said, "Yes! I want go Chinatown, see movie!"

I was nervous and excited, walking out of the academy with her. I tried to look calm and casual.

We went into a Chinese café across the street from the cinema. For the first time in my life I found myself sitting opposite a girl I liked. She looked so beautiful.

"You can call me Liz if you want. What about you? What do your friends call you?" she asked.

"Cunxin," I replied. "It mean 'keep my innocent heart.'"

"Cunxin, Cunxin, it's so beautiful," she murmured. "How old are you?"

"Nineteen," I replied.

"I'm eighteen." I could sense she had to concentrate on what I said.

"English hard. In English, you say go, goes, gone. In Chinese we say will go, go, and go yesterday, he go, she go, you go, I go, we all go."

She burst into laughter.

There were not many people in the cinema. I found it hard to concentrate with Elizabeth sitting next to me. I

240

wanted to know her better but I doubted she would show me any special interest. I was surprised when, after the movie, she agreed to have dinner with me.

We went to another small Chinese restaurant. We asked each other many questions and although we had difficulty understanding each other, we enjoyed being together. I ordered some authentic Chinese food—pig's intestines and sea slugs. That would impress her, I thought, but she seemed to have a rather small appetite. By the end of the evening I felt sad to part with her.

Before we approached Ben's apartment I told Elizabeth to stop the car. I didn't want the security guard to see us. If he told Ben I was having a relationship with an American, Ben would have to tell the Chinese consulate and I would be sent straight back to China.

Elizabeth stopped her car one block away from Ben's complex. "When can we see each other again?"

"Don't know," I replied. I reached out and we touched hands. I felt her breath. I felt hot blood rushing through each vein. We kissed. This was happening too fast. I needed time to think. So I quickly said good-bye and got out of her car.

"You'll call me, won't you?" she asked.

I nodded and walked to Ben's apartment.

❧

Elizabeth and I fell in love. I felt a great sense of responsibility for her, and great pride too. But I knew our secret relationship was dangerous. The only person I could think of to share my secret with was Lori, my "Big Ballerina." She had sometimes tried to persuade me to stay in America but I had always said no.

A few weeks later, one Sunday, Lori invited me to her house for a barbecue. I met her husband, Delworth, a Texas oil manager. I told them how much I liked Elizabeth and the sorrow I felt about returning to China. I didn't expect them to do anything about it but Delworth called the University of Texas and asked if they could recommend a good immigration lawyer. They suggested a lawyer called Charles Foster.

The following day Lori and Delworth took me to Charles Foster's office in downtown Houston. He said he had read about me in the newspaper. He said I could qualify on my artistic merits for a green card, which would enable me to stay and work in America. He also mentioned that the Chinese government recognized international marriage laws.

I remember feeling unsure, though not about my love for Elizabeth. I left that first meeting still very confused. I loved Elizabeth. And I couldn't go back and survive in a world with no freedom. Not anymore. But China was where my parents and family were, where my friends lived. I could still contribute a huge amount to Chinese ballet.

I realized I was torn between two possible lives.

# Elizabeth

I had been in Houston for eleven months. My secret relationship with Elizabeth was only a few months old. And I had to keep focused on my work.

I'd been rehearsing the *Le Corsaire* pas de deux one day with Suzanne, experimenting with a new, one-handed lift, when just before the end of our rehearsal there was a jerk in my shoulder joint and a sharp pain shot through my right arm. I caught Suzanne with my left hand on the way down, but I felt intense pain.

Ben and Suzanne were immediately concerned. I put an icepack on my shoulder joint. I knew I had dislocated it, and probably torn some tendons and muscles, but I didn't want to see a doctor. I didn't want Ben to think it was serious. He might take me out of the ballet.

My shoulder was swollen for days; I covered it up by wearing long-sleeved shirts. I couldn't do lifts properly and had to make different excuses. I knew that by continuing to practice I might make my injuries worse. But I also knew I needed to work harder if I was ever to reach the standard of Baryshnikov and Vasiliev. There was no way I was going to let injury slow me down.

Ben had choreographed a circle of six consecutive *double assemblé*, or double turns in the air, for my solo in *Le Corsaire*. I could barely do *one* well, let alone six. Every time my feet pushed off from the floor my body would twist in the air like a barbecued shrimp. "There's no point getting yourself injured," Ben said. "Let's change it."

"Please, give me few days," I begged, despite the pain of the injuries. I was angry with myself for not being able to do what Ben had in mind but there was a weekend coming up and I knew I could use it to practice. I locked myself in our studio for two days, practicing each movement and analyzing them in absolute detail—the angle of my leap, the timing, weight distribution, speed—everything. At times the pain was excruciating. I fell many times, but I didn't give up.

I made the breakthrough late on Sunday afternoon. I was elated. I truly believed that now nothing was impossible.

*Le Corsaire* was a huge success. Then, quite unexpectedly, Ben came onstage with a microphone in hand. He stood in front of the curtain and announced that he had the Chinese government's permission for me to stay in America longer and had promoted me to a soloist position with the Houston Ballet.

"This must be a dream," I thought. Senior Consul Zhang Zongshu from the Chinese consulate was in the audience that evening. He was very proud: I had brought glory to the Chinese people, he said. The Chinese government gave me permission to stay for an extra five months.

From then on I was a sort of celebrity in Houston. I was stopped by people in restaurants, shops, streets, even parking lots. Despite this instant stardom, I knew I would still have to work hard—I couldn't lose sight of my aim. My injuries gradually got better. I continued to stay with Ben and I continued to meet Elizabeth in secret. I felt guilty, as though I was betraying Ben and China, both at once. I wished I hadn't allowed myself to fall in love. Anyone I told about Elizabeth would be placed in a very dangerous situation with the Chinese government. I couldn't bear to put my family and friends in such a position. My only option was to stay quiet.

April 1981: less than a month to go before I was scheduled to return to China. The Houston Ballet's first major tour to New York was coming up and I was the understudy for the lonely, arrogant prince in John Cranko's *The Lady and the Fool*. Then one week before the performance in New York, Ben asked me to do a full rehearsal with the first-cast dancers. I was stunned.

The prince's first entrance was in the middle of a high-society ball. I had to enter at the far-back center stage and come down some steps with people on both sides of the stage standing back in silence and admiration. Walking down those steps was like walking on hot coals for me.

"Li, you're too nice," Ben said and stopped the pianist. "Go back and do it again. I want more arrogance."

I was shaking with embarrassment. I still had no idea what an arrogant prince would feel like. Ben made me repeat it over and over again. It paid off. My inhibitions went. I eventually enjoyed portraying this arrogant prince, who would have been considered evil in communist China. And here I was, portraying him with pride. I had made a fundamental shift in my dancing.

The two weeks in New York allowed me to really taste that city. Everywhere I went I made new friends. New York was full of artists. So many wonderful classes to choose from. One day, in a class at the School of American Ballet, I bumped into George Balanchine and Jerome Robbins, two of the most highly regarded choreographers in the world. For me, a peasant boy from Qingdao, it was amazing.

Another day, I remember peering into the American Ballet Theater's studio and seeing Baryshnikov doing a barre. I couldn't believe my eyes! This was the man I had admired for so long! How little he was! How could such great dancing come from such a small body? The following day, in the same studio, I found myself standing at the same barre as Gelsey Kirkland, the Sugarplum Fairy who danced with Baryshnikov in that *Nutcracker* video I'd watched in China. I was meeting people and experiencing things that I had only dreamed about in China.

❧

During the two weeks I was in New York, Elizabeth and I communicated through just one phone call. I missed her the whole time. My feelings about leaving her and going back to China became unbearable. I thought I had made up my mind to go back to China, but now I was wavering. What could China offer me? "The dance world is yours to explore and conquer in America," I told myself. "Elizabeth loves you dearly. Don't go back." But then I thought of my parents, my brothers, my friends back in China. What about Teacher Xiao and Teacher Zhang? What about Ben and his relationship with China? "They have done so much for you."

It was in this confused state of mind that I returned to Houston, only three days before my return to China. That afternoon I met Elizabeth two blocks away from Ben's apartment.

"I missed you!" she said, and immediately sensed my unease. "What's wrong?"

"Nothing wrong," I replied, but my heart was screaming.

We went to a gift shop in Chinatown where I bought Elizabeth a Chinese jade ring. "For our friendship," I said.

She looked at me tenderly. "Thank you," she replied.

My inner voice screamed: "You love her. Stay."

I called Lori. It was late afternoon. "Hi, Big Ballerina," I said. "I and Elizabeth, come talk with you?"

Lori's apartment was only half a block away from Elizabeth's. "I want marry Elizabeth!" I told Lori and Delworth as soon as we walked in.

Lori gave Elizabeth and me a passionate hug. She was so happy. Then she became more serious. "Have you told Ben?"

"No. I don't know how or when. He very angry when he find out, because he love China too much."

"Who cares about that?" Delworth barged in. "Let's have a wedding!"

"In two days I go back China. No time," I said.

"You could get married in a courthouse," Lori suggested. "It will only take a couple of hours. Delworth and I can be your witnesses."

So at ten the next morning Elizabeth and I made our vows as husband and wife in the county courthouse, with Lori and Delworth by our sides. Then the four of us walked out of the courthouse into a beautiful April day. "I'm married. I've married Elizabeth," I thought. And then immediately: "What have I done to Ben?"

"When are you going to tell Ben?" Elizabeth asked.

"Don't know. Big farewell party tonight! Maybe tomorrow," I replied. "Ben will be very angry. I don't know what he will do." I had done something behind Ben's back. Once more, happiness was overshadowed by guilt.

"Don't be afraid. We have each other," said Elizabeth. "You can dance anywhere."

"Yes, we have each other," I repeated.

There were over a hundred dancers and friends at the farewell party that night in the main dance studio. Everyone brought me presents and wished me happiness. I felt like screaming, "I'm married! I won't be going back to China tomorrow! Take your presents back!" But I couldn't. Instead I put on a pleasant face and continued the deception.

Elizabeth and I had our first dance together that night. "This is our wedding dance," she whispered. "Are you happy?"

I nodded but I felt very uncomfortable. Lori and Delworth were there too. The four of us pretended nothing special had happened.

The following morning, the day before I was to return to China, as soon as Ben and Zhang had gone out, Elizabeth, Delworth, and Lori arrived and loaded up my belongings. Then I made the phone call I dreaded most.

"Hello?" Ben answered.

"Ben, I want tell you something," I said straightaway. "I'm married. I not go back to China."

Silence.

Eventually: "Who?"

"Elizabeth Mackey," I replied.

"Elizabeth? You can't be married!" he was virtually shouting now. "You are going back to China! Tomorrow!"

"Ben, listen. I love Elizabeth; she is my wife."

"Li, I can't *believe* this! You are destroying everybody's lives. I won't *ever* be allowed back to China!"

My heart was torn by his words. I knew it was true. I would be responsible for creating so much pain for others. I knew Ben had been negotiating with the Chinese government to take some dancers to China—now his plans would be ruined. I felt I was being swept into a whirlpool. Only fate could determine the outcome.

Ben changed to a more persuasive, softer tone. "Li, why are you doing this? China is where you *belong*."

I felt our conversation was going nowhere. "Ben, I go now."

"Li, where are you?" he asked urgently.

It was no use going on. I hung up and buried my head in my hands.

Elizabeth, Lori, and Delworth looked very concerned.

I tried to repeat everything Ben had said. I knew one thing for sure. There wouldn't be a future for me at the Houston Ballet. It broke my heart. The only comfort was Elizabeth's love and Lori and Delworth's friendship.

The phone rang. It was Ben.

"Li's not here," Delworth said and hung up.

Another five minutes passed.

Then a loud knock at the door. It was Clare Duncan. "Hello, Delworth. Can I have a word with Li?"

"Li's not here," Delworth repeated.

"Are you sure?" Clare inquired, then left.

The phone rang again.

"Delworth, I know Li is there!" said Ben. "Clare saw his luggage in your car." He paused. "Li's situation is serious. I need to speak to him urgently."

Delworth gave me the phone.

"Ohh . . . Li!" Ben started to sob. "I've lost everything! Consul Zhang thinks I've masterminded this whole thing. They think it's all my fault. You have ruined everything! I'll never be allowed back into China now!"

"I'm sorry, Ben. What you want me say?" I asked.

"I want you to say that this is all a mistake and that you *will* go back to China. Nothing will change if you go back now. I have spoken to Consul Zhang. You'll still be allowed to come back to America."

"If you want live in China, you go," I said.

"Li, the least you can do for me is explain all this to the consulate! Tell them I had nothing to do with it."

"Yes, I will do that," I replied.

"Then I'll tell Consul Zhang that you will meet them at the consulate," he said, and he hung up.

"I don't think you should go," Elizabeth said.

"Already, I say yes to Ben. I will go." I was determined.

"I think we should call Charles Foster," Delworth said, and I knew this was the most sensible idea.

Charles was surprised to hear from me. I hadn't

spoken to him since our meeting twelve weeks earlier. He congratulated me on our marriage but when I told him that Ben had asked me to go to the Chinese consulate, he strongly advised against it. "The consulate is considered Chinese territory. Better to meet on neutral ground."

"Is dangerous to meet in consulate?" I asked nervously.

"It could be dangerous," he replied.

I quickly called Ben back and told him I wanted to meet the Chinese officials at a restaurant instead.

"Li, *you* call them," he told me.

So I did. I called Consul Zhang. He sounded surprisingly calm and pleasant. "Cunxin, come to the consulate. I only want to have a little chat with you. No more than five minutes. Then you will be free to go and enjoy your happy life with your bride."

Delworth drove Lori, Elizabeth, and me to the Chinese consulate on Montrose Boulevard. When we arrived Charles was already at the consulate gate. As soon as we entered, the big metal door clanged shut behind us.

My heart sank. I should have listened to Charles. I felt like a prisoner of China already.

# Defection

We were taken to a meeting room where Ben, Clare Duncan, and Jack, the Houston Ballet Company's lawyer, were already waiting. Consul Zhang was there with his wife, and several other consulate officials. The only one missing was the consul general himself. They seemed relaxed and friendly. Ben was clearly furious. He wouldn't even look at me.

It was about six in the evening by now.

I looked around the room. It was a big square with black-and-white Chinese landscapes on the walls.

The atmosphere was tense.

We were offered tea and soft drinks and there was a lot of small talk about China and the improving relationship between the two countries. Nobody was talking about why we were there at all! I was very scared. I couldn't stand the suspense much longer.

Then one of the officials asked Charles and Jack to

speak with him, alone, in a room down the hall. I wanted Charles to stay but he gave me a reassuring look.

But to those of us left, it seemed as though the consulate officials were keeping the conversation going, trying to distract us, while they gradually eliminated my friends from the room. People disappeared one by one. Each time a friend left I squeezed Elizabeth's hand tighter and tighter. It wasn't long before only Consul Zhang, Clare, Elizabeth, myself, and two officials remained.

Eventually Consul Zhang asked everyone, except me, to go to another room. He wanted a private conversation.

Elizabeth refused. We begged Clare to stay with us, but the two officials simply shoved her outside.

Then four security guards stormed in, heading straight for Elizabeth and me.

We screamed. Clare looked back and screamed too.

It took only a few seconds for the four highly trained Chinese guards to separate me from Elizabeth. I was completely helpless against them. They quickly grabbed my arms and legs, carried me to the top floor, and locked me into a small room.

I was struggling to breathe. I was scared. Truly scared.

Downstairs, Charles Foster realized what was happening. He demanded to see his client.

From then on, Charles said later, the atmosphere changed completely. In a very strident voice the consulate official ordered Charles to sit. He was on Chinese territory and was expected to follow orders. The two employees who were serving drinks dropped their trays and assumed a defensive stance, blocking the door. Charles charged forward but was shoved aside as he tried to get through. He could hear my voice yelling from the other room—"Help, they are taking me! Help, they are taking me!" By the time Charles and Jack got back to the main room everyone was there except me.

From my room on the top floor I could hear the guards talking outside the door. I was terrified. I remembered the executions I had witnessed as a child during the Cultural Revolution, and I saw my own death flash in front of my eyes. I felt desperately alone. Nobody could save me. It was just a matter of time before they stuck a gun to my head or forced me back to China where I would suffer a humiliating death.

I tried to think about my niang and her sweet laughter. I tried to think about my dia and his humble stories. I tried to think about Elizabeth, the scent of her perfume. I remembered the Bandit and our blood brothers' poem, but I couldn't hold on to any one comforting thread.

The door opened. Consul Zhang came into the room. He sat in front of me and attempted a smile, but he seemed very sad. He looked straight into my eyes, like a chess player trying to figure out a strategy. We sat there just looking at each other. I was perspiring profusely. I couldn't stand this silence. If I sat there any longer my heart would explode. I had to do something! What to say to Consul Zhang? What *was* there to say? I was a defector, the most hated traitor of all.

Consul Zhang finally broke the silence. "Cunxin, do you understand what you have done?" he asked.

"I love Elizabeth and I married her. Is this against the law?" I replied.

"Yes! What you have done is against your government's wishes and is illegal in China! You're a Chinese citizen! *Your* government doesn't recognize your marriage."

"Consul Zhang, my lawyer, Mr. Foster, told me that China *does* recognize international marriage law. I married here in America and American law should be observed."

He was incensed. "The foreigners will use you and dump you like a piece of trash! It's not too late to change your mind. Just tell Elizabeth that you have made a mistake and want to walk away from it."

"No," I said, "I want to spend the rest of my life with Elizabeth."

"We won't recognize your marriage as legitimate. *You* don't decide what you're going to do with your life, the Communist Party does! You're a Chinese citizen. You follow Chinese laws, not American laws."

By now I was angry. "If you think Mr. Foster has informed me wrongly, let's ask him about it," I said.

Consul Zhang looked perplexed. "Mr. Foster and your friends have left. They are disgusted with what you have done! You are alone. *We're* your friends. Everything will be forgiven if you go back to China as planned."

I didn't believe for a moment what Consul Zhang said about my friends. They must have been thrown out of the consulate. I knew the Chinese government would promise me anything to get me back to China.

There was a knock on the door and Consul Zhang left for a brief discussion with another man. I could hear whispers but I couldn't make out what they were saying. Then Consul Zhang came back. He was trying hard to control his anger. "I want you to think about what we have just discussed. I'll come back soon."

I felt a sense of relief when he closed the door. I needed to gather my courage. I felt exhausted but I knew this was only the beginning of a long, nerve-racking night.

A few minutes later one of the vice-consuls general entered, an older man. He was very friendly and offered me something to drink. I politely refused. He began to try to convince me to go back to China, listing all the benefits there would be for my family. "Think of your parents and all your brothers back home! You don't want to create any problem for them, do you?"

This was my greatest fear, that something terrible might happen to my family because of what I had done.

"I left my family when I was eleven. I have nothing to do

with them and they have nothing to do with me," I tried to tell him. I couldn't implicate my family in this.

"You are the property of China," the vice-consul general continued. "We have given you everything. We have the power to do anything we want with you. We don't want to lose our star dancer! You simply *have* to listen to what we say. The party knows what's good for you. Have you forgotten what the party has done for you?"

I remembered the years and years of lies about the West. I thought of Minister Wang who had refused to see me about my return to America. I thought of my lack of freedom in China, the desperate poverty that they had made sound so rich and glorious. "I don't want to talk about the party," I said.

"Who helped you to get married? Is it Ben? Is it someone in the American government?" he asked suddenly.

"No one has helped me. Would I have come to the consulate tonight if the Americans had helped me? Would they have advised me to come?" I asked.

The conversation with the vice-consul general went on for another half hour. Then a different consulate official replaced him for another half hour of interrogation and persuasion. It was like musical chairs. Every half hour another official would take over the interrogation. Each left without making any progress. In a strange way, I felt calmer and stronger as time went on.

During the interrogations I touched the scar on my

arm, the one I received as a baby, the one that caused so much anxiety for my parents and that had now become a symbol of my niang's love. When I touched it I could feel her love. It gave me comfort. It gave me courage.

I didn't regret what I had done. In a strange way I felt at peace with myself. Elizabeth was my first love. Our marriage was not a marriage of convenience. I knew I could even have stayed in America on my own artistic merits. Charles had told me this at our very first meeting. But still I felt a strong sense of sorrow for my parents.

I felt the tears pushing upward through my throat. My poor dear niang. She had suffered enough hardship already. I thought of the sorrow she would feel if she never saw me again. Oh, how much I loved her!

I thought too of my teachers who had invested so much of their time and effort in me, hoping that I would one day put Chinese ballet on the world map. Their hopes would be dashed. I would never see them again. But I was determined not to allow the consulate officials to see my tears or sense my weakness.

❧

Downstairs, in the main room, everyone was shaken. The consulate officials changed their approach and went back to their pleasantries again, offering everyone drinks. Charles told me later that he sat there, bewildered, until he could stand it no longer. "My client was just dragged out of here

259

and I am not leaving until you have released him! You are in violation of US law!"

"I don't understand, Mr. Foster," Consul Zhang spoke up with genuine surprise. "You just told us that you strongly support good US-China relations. What is good for China and for the United States is for Li to return to China. If he does not, US-China relations will be harmed. So will the Houston Ballet and their planned tour to the People's Republic of China."

"While we may all agree with you about what's good for US-China relations, there's one problem with what you say. In the United States, Li gets to make that decision." Charles was concerned about my safety. He feared they would hold me through the night and then take me to the airport and fly me out of America the following morning.

Despite his disappointment, Ben joined my friends and refused to leave the consulate without me. So the consulate officials turned the lights out. The tea, soft drinks, and crackers were withdrawn. About twenty minutes later the officials came back into the room. Polite persuasion changed to cold, threatening words.

Ben and my friends continued to resist.

By now, rumors about my detention at the consulate had started to spread. Two people in particular wanted to find out the truth: Anne Holmes and Carl Cunningham, dance critics for the *Houston Chronicle* and the *Houston Post*. They'd planned to interview me that night, but as time dragged on they had discovered that I was being held at the consulate against my will.

Hours passed. People were beginning to gather at the side entrance to the consulate, Anne and Carl among them.

⁂

At one o'clock in the morning, after many hours of interrogation, I was collapsing with hunger and exhaustion. My head was throbbing. I couldn't think anymore. I hadn't had anything since breakfast the previous morning. I asked for something to eat.

They found me some leftover fried rice and a Tsingtao beer: at least I would taste something from my hometown before I left this world, I thought.

After my meal they wanted to resume the interrogation. I told them that my brain couldn't take any more. "Please, just leave me alone." If they wanted to kill me they should do it now. I had made up my mind. I wasn't going back to China.

To my surprise they agreed to stop their interrogation. They assigned one of the guards to sleep in the room and keep an eye on me. We both twisted and turned all night.

About the same time, Charles had his final discussion with Anne and Carl outside the consulate. They wanted to know all the details. This was a front-page story. Charles asked them to withhold writing anything until the matter was resolved. They said they appreciated that, but they had a greater duty to the public and they had deadlines to meet. Charles went back inside and asked to use the telephone. First he rang renowned federal judge Woodrow Seals. It was about two in the morning by then.

Charles briefly explained the emergency and Judge Seals told him that he would meet him at the federal courthouse at 6 a.m. along with one of the chief justices of Texas. Charles then called his legal assistant to help draw up documents.

Then, unknown to the consulate officials, Charles made another crucial call to the US State Department. He said this was a critical matter. The US government should act. Charles knew the US State Department had internal regulations about the forcible repatriation of foreign nationals, based on previous experience, particularly when it came to communist countries.

At this point the Chinese officials became suspicious and told Charles that he could no longer use their phones. In any event, he had to leave the consulate to help draft the legal documents. There were only a few hours left until morning and he wanted to speed things along.

After Charles left the consulate the Chinese officials demanded all the other Westerners leave the consulate at once. They refused to leave until they saw me safe and sound. This irritated the Chinese even more. They cut off the phone and turned off the lights once more.

When Charles left the consulate the morning papers were already out on the streets. The headlines read: CHINESE

CONSULATE HOLDING EIGHT AMERICANS HOSTAGE. He returned to his office, then went to the federal courthouse with the finished legal documents, ready for signing.

Federal Judge Woodrow Seals and Chief Justice John Singleton were there as arranged.

"There's not much time," Charles told them.

⁂

Once the documents were signed, Charles phoned Chase Untermeyer, executive assistant to Vice President George Bush. "Chase," he said, "Vice President Bush's wife, Barbara, is a trustee of the Houston Ballet. The vice president should know the Chinese consulate is holding a Houston Ballet dancer, Li Cunxin, against his will." Charles knew the vice president would take appropriate action. Chase immediately contacted Vice President Bush.

Charles then returned to the consulate with a federal marshall to serve both court orders, one ordering the consul general to produce me, the other stopping him from removing me from the country. The handful of people waiting outside had grown. One man walked up to Charles and whispered in his ear. He was FBI. "The consulate is surrounded," he said. "There is no way they can take Li out."

Charles knocked on the door of the consulate, accompanied by the US marshall, trying to serve the court orders. "Go away," said an official, "there is no one here."

For the rest of the day Charles went to and from the consulate but he was not allowed inside. He received many phone calls both from the federal court and from Washington. The number of FBI agents outside the consulate began to grow.

Charles then received another call, from the White House. President Reagan was inquiring about the status of the case. Then the State Department called and asked Charles to go back to the consulate and tell them to reconnect their phones. The Chinese embassy in Washington was trying to contact them to give them instructions.

Charles returned to the consulate around 4 p.m. and by five o'clock he was again talking to Consul Zhang. Consul Zhang was distraught. He asked Charles once more, did he *have* to release me?

"Yes. If you don't release Li, it will only get worse."

All the major networks were outside with television cameras. In my room at the top of the consulate, I was completely unaware of what was happening.

Soon after 5 p.m. Consul Zhang returned to my room. "Cunxin, for your own good, and for the last time: will you go back to China?"

"Here is the turning point of my life," I thought. I was prepared for the worst. "No, I won't go back. Do whatever you like with me."

He looked at me long and hard. Finally he said sadly, "I'm sorry you have chosen this road. I believe you will regret it later. I'm sad we have lost you to America. You're now a man without a country and a people. There are many reporters outside. I want to warn you, what you say to them now or in the future will have a direct effect on you and your family back in China. We will be watching you."

I could hardly believe what I had heard. I was going to be *free*.

Suddenly, I felt only compassion toward Consul Zhang. I understood that he only represented the government's desires, what was best for China and the Communist Party. Unlike me, he *had* to go back and would probably never manage to get out again. He had been kind to me the whole time I was in Houston.

"I'm sorry, Consul Zhang," I said sincerely.

He looked at me with a barely detectable hint of empathy and led me downstairs to Elizabeth and Charles.

I kissed and hugged Elizabeth and told her that I loved her. I thanked Charles for saving my life. He was a man of great integrity.

I didn't want to say anything to the reporters but Charles knew they wouldn't leave me alone until I did. So, I walked out of the Chinese Consulate and faced a sea of microphones, flashing lights, and cameras, and with Elizabeth by my side I managed a few simple words: "I am very happy to be able to stay with my wife and in America. I would like to do nice things for China and American art in the future."

I could hardly believe it. I was going to be free . . .

# Afterword

My new life with Elizabeth began like an East-meets-West fairy tale, but it didn't work out the way we both had hoped, even though we loved and cared for each other. We were too young. My poor English prevented us from deeply understanding each other. We faced the harsh reality of enormous cultural differences, and our marriage eventually failed. We suffered greatly and I felt terribly alone in the world. I had no one to go to, and no home to go to. My parents and family in China were totally cut off from me. I didn't even know whether my defection had caused them further hardship in life, or difficulties for them with the Chinese government. I feared for their safety. There was no way back for me.

I didn't blame Elizabeth for our failed marriage. I blamed myself, and I blamed fate. I felt like a total failure. I shrank into my own protective cocoon. The only way I could pull myself out of my misery was to pour myself into dancing. Ballet was my salvation.

Within a year I was promoted to principal dancer status at the Houston Ballet. I danced many leading roles, in most of the classical ballets: *Swan Lake*, *Sleeping Beauty*, *Romeo and Juliet*, and countless contemporary ballets. I toured and performed in many countries, learned about and experienced different cultures, but I didn't stop there. I continued to work hard. I gave everything I had to each role I danced and acted. Teacher Xiao's stories continued to inspire and motivate me. I even won a bronze and two silver medals at international ballet competitions in Russia, Japan, and America. They were like the Olympics of the dance world. Many ballet companies invited me to perform with them as a guest star, and my dance career went from strength to strength.

Then I had a career-shattering accident at my last international ballet competition in Moscow. Just minutes before I was to dance in the first round, I took a near fatal fall, injuring my back during one of the big leaps. I didn't realize how severe the injury was, so, with determination and perseverance, I finished the competition and received a bronze medal. Later, I was diagnosed with two herniated discs in my lower spine.

The injury was an enormous setback in my dance career, and in my life. I was devastated. I felt frightened by the prospect of never being able to dance again. Ballet was all I had known since the age of eleven. It was my passion, my life. How could I, once again, be left on my own with an unknown future? Now I was like a soaring bird who had been suddenly shot down, a caged tiger once again.

I was put on bed rest for several months by the doctor. My frustration and despair were beyond description. I was told by the doctor that my chances of ever being able to dance again were very slim. Many people doubted that I would ever make it back onstage, but I believed that if there was a way, then I would find it. I would not take no for an answer.

I knew the only chance for recovery was to be as disciplined with my rehabilitation as I had been with my dancing. I would need all the perseverance and determination I had. It greatly tested my self-belief, and I fought with self-doubt on a daily basis.

Luckily, by then, I had met Mary McKendry, a new principal dancer of the Houston Ballet, an exceptional dancer in her own right. She brought me books and led me along the road toward discovering the literary world.

After months of intense rehabilitation and hard work, I finally made it back onstage. I went on to dance for another thirteen years.

Despite the success of my dancing career, I constantly thought of my beloved parents and brothers. I missed them. I worried about them. Soon after my defection, I wrote to them, but received no reply, and this added even more fear to my already heavy heart. The guilt I felt was immense. I secretly prayed for their well-being and safety. The thought of never being able to see my niang, my dia, and my six brothers again made my heart bleed over and over. I tried hard to suppress my guilt, my worries, and the sadness deep in my heart. I had to keep going forward.

⚬⚬⚬

In 1984, I was dancing the role of the prince on the opening night of Ben's *Swan Lake* at the Kennedy Center in Washington DC. Vice President George Bush and his wife, Barbara, were present. Ben had made them aware of my situation with China. During the intermission, the Bushes invited the Chinese ambassador and the cultural attaché to their private box and asked them to help me. I discovered then that the Chinese cultural attaché was Wang Zicheng, the man who had briefed Zhang Weiqiang and me at the Ministry of Culture in China before we'd left China for America that first time in 1979. The Chinese embassy officials agreed to help, to my great surprise, and a letter arrived a few months later from Wang Zicheng. The Chinese government had given my parents permission to leave China to visit me in America.

I held that letter tight in my hand as that night, trembling with joy, I dialed my old village phone number.

First I heard my brothers' excited voices, all fighting to speak to me first. They had run to the commune phone ahead of my parents. In the middle of my conversation with my youngest brother, Jing Tring, another voice spoke urgently into the receiver.

It was my niang. At last!

"Is it really you, my sixth son . . . ?" Her voice choked up, and she started to sob. "Oh, my son . . . !"

I told her that they had permission to come and visit me in America. She didn't believe me at first. Then, just before we ended our conversation, I said, "Niang . . . before you go, I just want to tell you . . . I love you!"

This was the first time I'd ever told her that. How many times I'd wished I'd said it to her before I went to America!

There was silence.

Then all I heard was my niang sobbing.

⋘❦⋙

Charles Foster helped with my parents' visa applications. My parents were scheduled to arrive in Houston on the opening night of *Nutcracker*. It was December 18, 1984. I spent the entire day in the studio and theater practicing. Concentrating on the performance was the only thing that helped my anxiety about my parents. Everything felt strange and new that day. Even my makeup brush felt unsteady. My hands trembled and I could hear my heart thumping loudly.

I went onstage and felt the intense heat of the spotlights. How would my parents react to these bright lights, to the thousands of people clapping in the audience? They had never seen me perform. They had never even been in a theater before. I wondered, would they be proud of me?

It was time to start, but the curtain didn't rise. I was

told that people were stuck in heavy traffic and the performance would be delayed.

The truth was, however, that my parents' plane was late. By the time they arrived it was twenty minutes past curtain time and I was a nervous wreck.

Word spread quickly through the audience about my parents' arrival. Houstonians were well aware of my story, so when my parents were finally ushered into the theater, the whole audience burst into applause.

My poor niang! My poor dia! They had never been away from Qingdao before. They had just had their first car ride, train ride, and airplane experience all in one day. And now here they were, suddenly faced with the blinding lights of a grand theater and a sea of people applauding them.

"Six years! Six long years! Finally I'm going to see my son. My heart is so hot, it burns with joy and pride!" my niang kept saying.

I was told of my parents' arrival only moments before the applause erupted from the audience. My whole being burst with happiness. I wanted to soar into the air. I wanted to see them then, at that very moment, but the performance was about to start and I would have to wait.

The audience was ecstatic that night. People applauded me when I first came onstage. They too wanted me to dance well, to dance well for my parents.

Everything went seamlessly. The lifts felt light, the partnering felt effortless. My nerves were there, yet under control, and they in turn became my endless source of energy. My leaps were high. It felt as if I was flying like a bird, gliding through the open sky, and if the music had allowed it, I would have stayed in the air all night. My pirouettes felt like I was turning in silk, smooth and secure. I felt totally free. It was not hard work, it was sheer joy. All those years of one-legged stair hopping, of pirouetting in candlelight, of torn hamstrings and painful injuries all came together in that show. When the curtain came down at the end of act one, I knew I had given one of my best performances and I had done it in front of my parents. The dream I had once been too afraid to dream had at last come true.

During intermission, Ben brought my niang and my dia onstage.

It had been six years since I had set eyes on them. They wore Mao's suits buttoned all the way up to their necks, my niang in gray and my dia in dark blue. They looked so proper, so stiff. My memories of them didn't match. They looked older too, especially my niang. Her black hair had turned gray and the many years of harsh living had obviously taken their toll. Her face was more wrinkled and now she wore a pair of black-rimmed oversized glasses.

The three of us, in tears, simply hugged each other tight. Nobody spoke for a long time. My niang took her handkerchief out and it was already soaked with tears. "Don't cry! Don't cry! It's all right now!" she kept saying.

I wanted that moment to linger on and on and on. I had longed for her comfort for so many years.

By the time I went back to my dressing room to change for the second act, I realized that nearly all my makeup had been wiped off by my niang's handkerchief. But I didn't care. I had felt my niang's adoring love and tender touch once more.

After the performance, my niang and my dia came backstage again. They watched people congratulate me for the performance, and I could see the pride in my parents' eyes.

Finally, my dia, the man of few words, could contain himself no longer. "Why didn't you wear any *pants?*" he said. He had never seen anyone wearing tights before.

That night, with my parents sleeping just a few yards away, I tucked myself under the blankets and slept like a baby. No more nightmares now.

Mary McKendry and I were married in October 1987, and on June 3, 1988, we arrived at the Beijing Airport, met by my blood brother the Bandit and my violinist friend Fengtian and their wives. There was so much joy for us all. It was nine years since we last saw each other.

I was now allowed to visit my old school, the Beijing Dance Academy. Teacher Xiao and Zhang Shu met me at the gate. We could only shake hands and looked at each other through tear-filled eyes. They asked me to perform for them, and I did. I could see in their eyes that they were proud of what I'd achieved.

A few days later, we went to Qingdao to see my family. As we approached our village, massive firecrackers exploded and a huge crowd gathered around us. It was an emotional reunion for us all. Mary was welcomed into our family and quickly won all their hearts. All of my brothers were married now except Jing Tring. He was to marry a lovely young lady while we were there.

The wedding day was a beautiful but hot summer day. During the height of the party, Mary and I danced for the guests in our small courtyard, and for most of them, this was the first time they'd ever seen ballet. We hummed the music and danced for our loved ones, and our adoring audience clapped and cheered our every lift and movement. It was one of our most rewarding performances ever.

When the moment came for Mary and I to bid farewell to my niang, my dia, and my brothers, Mary was an emotional mess and my heart was a big twisted knot. It felt just like the time when I'd first left for the Beijing Dance Academy, sixteen years earlier. Leaving my beloved niang would always be just too hard. Even the family rock, my dia, tried hard to control his emotions when we finally shook hands in farewell. As our truck pulled away, I saw him wiping tears away from his face.

I was going home. But I was leaving home too. I was closing a full circle within my heart. The longest chapter of my life had finally come to an end. I thought of my beloved ones. Now they didn't have to eat dried yams or tree bark. Now they had better food to eat. Now their living standard had improved considerably.

But Mary and I couldn't stop comparing our life in the West to my family's life in Qingdao, and at times I was overwhelmed with guilt. Ever since I had been selected for the Beijing Dance Academy, I had felt this guilt, this burden, this sense of responsibility for my family. I wished all of my brothers could have had the opportunities I'd had, but from the bottom of my sad heart I knew it was not to be. I was the one who had to fulfill my family's dreams. Mary and I had given each of them as much money as we could afford, but I knew, deep in my heart, that it didn't matter how much I gave them, because it would only ever provide them with temporary help. What they needed most was the one thing I couldn't give them—the opportunity to get out of the well. Maybe, just maybe, now for the first time in their lives, there was a glimpse of hope under Deng Xiaoping's leadership. I had gone back home and had expected to leave them feeling light and optimistic. Instead I was leaving with a confused heart.

I sat on the plane and watched the thick clouds pass beneath. I had no desire to sleep. I could think only of my family. My family and friends lived so simply in China, but they made their happiness in their own way.

Mary was sleeping now. I looked at her kind and peaceful face. I felt truly blessed to have found her, to have her by my side, to continue our journey together. I felt truly blessed to have my family and friends. Their courage and love had always propelled me forward.

I had no idea what would happen next in our lives. My guilt at leaving my family in China began to be replaced with excitement. The road I had traveled so far had had so many detours. Nothing had been smooth or easy. I knew the road ahead wouldn't be smooth or easy either, but the possibilities of the world were so vast. The pursuit of my dreams, the determination to achieve them, had given me a miraculous career and an enchanted life. No matter what lay ahead or behind, I had the love of my niang, my dia, my brothers, and my friends. I had Mary as my lifelong companion.

I looked out of the aircraft window into the darkening sky. I saw myself as a small boy, running barefoot through the commune fields. I saw myself as a Red Guard, and I saw myself as Mao's last dancer. I thought of my niang's extraordinary courage and unlimited love. I thought of my journey with all its twists and turns, and of how that journey had led me to the most precious thing of all, my freedom.

～❧～

Back in America, our dance careers continued. Mary danced even better than before. Life seemed perfect. Our first child, Sophie, was born in 1989. She brought such happiness and laughter into our lives. Then, when Sophie was eighteen months old, we discovered that she was profoundly deaf. We were devastated. Our beloved daughter would never hear music, would never hear all the sounds we took for granted. She wouldn't be able to communicate to the speaking world. Faced with the enormous amount of work ahead of us in helping Sophie, Mary decided to give up her dance career and devote all her time to teaching Sophie to speak. I knew Mary's sacrifice would end her dance career forever. I was heartbroken for her, because I knew how much she loved ballet. She had spent her entire life perfecting her art form.

With Mary's total dedication and the help of an Australian invention called the cochlear implant, Sophie made rapid improvements. She is now fifteen years old and studying in a mainstream school, learning piano, ballet, tap, and jazz. It's impossible to adequately describe how we lived through this difficult ordeal. Sophie is our miracle child.

Our second child, Thomas, was born in 1992, and our third child, Bridie, arrived in 1997. Both of them were born with normal hearing.

In 1995, after dancing with the Houston Ballet for nearly sixteen years, I decided to join the Australian Ballet as a principal artist and so we moved to Melbourne. This was a very difficult decision. It was emotionally hard to leave the Houston Ballet, which had been like a family to me for over fifteen years. Professionally, it was going to be a new challenge in a new country, but for Mary it meant returning to her homeland for the first time since she'd left Australia to study ballet in London at the age of seventeen.

My farewell performance with the Houston Ballet actually took place in China. It was the first time I had been allowed to perform in China, the place where it had all begun for me. I danced Romeo in Ben's *Romeo and Juliet*, and the Central TV of China broadcast the opening night live—to five hundred million people throughout the country. I watched tears of pride running down Teacher Xiao's face. I saw the pride in the Bandit's eyes, and I heard Fengtian and my teachers, classmates, and the entire audience cheer. My only sadness was that Zhang Shu wasn't there—he had died from a heart attack a few years before.

The Australian Ballet was a new challenge for me. I danced in Australia for three more years, and these were some of the most satisfying years of my whole career. The Australian audience embraced me warmly from the beginning.

During my last few years of dancing I began to study finance on the weekend and in the evening to prepare myself for a career transition. Now I am a manager at one of the largest stock brokerage firms in Australia.

And what of the others in my story?

Ben came to my last performance in Sydney in April

1999, and I went to his farewell gala in Houston—he had especially choreographed a solo for me to perform. Mary is still the love of my life and is currently teaching and coaching at the Australian Ballet. Elizabeth remarried and has a son. Charles Foster remains a close friend: we are godfathers to each other's children.

Zhang Weiqiang also left China for the West and danced in both Japan and Canada for some years. Teacher Xiao has become one of the most respected teachers and choreographers in China. The Bandit and Fengtian have left their artistic professions and become businessmen in China, like over a billion others there. All of my brothers are doing well in their own businesses and their living standards continue to improve.

In 2003, I made a surprise visit to my family in China and showed up at my parents' doorstep quite unannounced. My niang was cooking in the kitchen. Upon seeing me, she dropped her wok flipper and could only manage to utter, "Ah! Ah! You! It's you!" She threw her arms around me and hugged me tight.

# A Short Note on the
# Long History of China

China represents the oldest surviving civilization in the world. The country's written records date back 4,000–5,000 years. China is renowned for scholarship (the world's first university was founded there in 124 BC), for inventions and building and engineering achievements—and for the world's first tea plantations. Confucius, a Chinese scholar who lived 550 years before Jesus, founded the religious philosophy of Confucianism, which became the state religion of China for 2,000 years. China's painting, porcelain, and sculpture date from ancient times, as does its calligraphy, poetry, drama, and the world's first novel. Chinese inventions include paper, ink and printing, gunpowder, and fireworks—and the humble wheelbarrow, nicknamed "the Wooden Ox." Famous building and engineering projects include the Great Wall of China and a vast canal network.

From 221 BC to AD 1911, China was ruled by twenty-four successive imperial family dynasties. Peasants, the poor people of the countryside who worked for the landowners, made up 90 percent of China's population, and each of the dynasties was eventually overthrown by peasant rebellions. Throughout this time there were also civil wars and foreign invasions.

In 1911, after the fall of the last dynasty, the Manchu, the Chinese Republic was founded by the revolutionary leader Sun Yat-sen. In 1921, the Chinese Communist Party was founded. An early member was young Mao Zedong, son of a peasant. In 1927, two years after Sun Yat-sen died, General Chiang Kaishek, who was opposed to the Communist Party, became the head of the Chinese Nationalist (Guomindang) government, supported by the more prosperous sections of Chinese society.

Japan invaded northern China in 1931, occupied Manchuria, and gradually forced the nationalist army into the interior. An army of communist partisans also resisted the Japanese invasion, but the two Chinese armies were opposed to each other. In 1934, the communists, pursued by the nationalists, were forced from their base in South China to the North, traveling 7,500 miles across the mountains. This epic journey is known as "The Long March." Almost 100,000 communists set out on The Long March: thousands perished along the way, and less than 8,000 reached their destination. In 1935, Mao Zedong, hero of The Long March, became leader of the Communist Party.

When World War II broke out in 1939, the Allied powers forced the nationalists and the communists to fight together against the Japanese. This situation lasted until 1945, when Japan surrendered to the Allies. Civil war broke out again between the two Chinese armies and continued until 1949, when Chiang Kaishek's defeated nationalists finally sought refuge on the island of Taiwan. The victorious Chairman Mao Zedong proclaimed the People's Republic of China in Beijing on October 1, 1949.

Then Mao announced the strategy of the Great Leap Forward. He founded People's Communes, based on communist Russia's soviet policies. Throughout China this strategy, which lasted a decade, led to chaos, economic disaster, and famine. In addition, any form of religion was abolished under communist rule. For a short time Mao fell from power, but soon regained it. In 1966, he proclaimed the Great Proletarian Cultural Revolution. His new message was spread across the land by his Red Guards, who killed or imprisoned numerous scholars and artists, and destroyed ancient buildings, artifacts, and gardens. The Cultural Revolution lasted until 1976. Chairman Mao's communist philosophy was set out in the Little Red Book, which every schoolchild had to read. Then Madame Mao, a former actor, was placed in charge of a new program of theater and ballet, with the aim of using these arts as propaganda for her husband's communist philosophy.

American president Richard Nixon made a successful

inaugural visit to Beijing in 1972, four years before the death of Chairman Mao. After Mao's death, Deng Xiaoping gradually led China to a more liberal way of life, with family-based farming and limited private enterprise. In 1980, China took her place in a number of international organizations. The new leaders of communist China always feared counterrevolutionary action, and in 1989 the Western world was horrified by the massacre of students who took part in a protest at Beijing's famous Tiananmen Square. However, by 1992 economic reforms were introduced that improved the lives of the Chinese people, who began to look forward to a new era of prosperity.

Li Cunxin's story, which takes place between 1961 and 1981, during and immediately after the time of Chairman Mao, presents a vivid impression of those difficult years.

*Barbara Ker Wilson*

# Li Cunxin and China

## A Historic Time Line

**1893**  Mao Zedong born

**1911**  Fall of the last dynasty, the Manchu
Chinese Republic founded by Sun Yat-sen

**1921**  Chinese Communist Party founded

**1927**  General Chiang Kaishek becomes leader of
Guomindang government

**1931**  Japan invades northern China

**1934**  The Long March

**1935**  Mao becomes leader of Communist Party


**1939–1945  World War II**


**1946–1949**  Civil war in China

**1946**  Li Cunxin's parents' marriage

**1949**  Victorious Chairman Mao proclaims People's
Republic of China in Beijing

**1958**  The Great Leap Forward

**1961**   Li Cunxin born

**1966–1976**   The Cultural Revolution
**1967**   *The Quotes of Chairman Mao*, also known as the
Little Red Book, published
**1972**   President Nixon visits China
Li goes to Beijing for the first time
**1976**   Zhou Enlai, premier of China, dies. Mao dies.
Madame Mao and the Gang of Four arrested.
Deng Xiaoping becomes the leader of the
Communist Party of China

**1972–1979**   **Li Cunxin studies at the Beijing
Dance Academy**

**1974**   Li Cunxin becomes member of the Communist
Youth Party
**1979**   Li Cunxin graduates from Beijing Dance Academy
and goes to the United States for the first time.
Returns to America in November 1979
**1981**   Li marries Elizabeth Mackey. Defection to the West
**1987**   Li marries Mary McKendry
**1988**   Mary and Li visit China together for the first time
**1989**   Tiananmen Square Massacre
Sophie, Li's first daughter, born
**1995**   Li Cunxin moves to Melbourne, Australia
**1999**   Li retires from ballet

# Writing and Pronouncing
# Chinese Words in English

Chinese and English are two very distinct languages, each with its own written form. As we learn more about each other's cultures, the translations between our languages continue to evolve. For example, Beijing, the capital city of China, was once pronounced "Peking" by non-Chinese speakers.

Both Chinese and English have their own sets of sounds that are difficult to match up exactly with each other. In Chinese, sounds like "hs," "ts," and "zh" are very common, but they seem unusual for English speakers. Since there is no direct translation between written Chinese characters and the alphabet used to write English, many sounds from spoken Chinese are not easily spelled. We do our best to write Chinese words phonetically, so that the letters form the sounds that are made when it's spoken. Following is a phonetic guide to the major people and places in Li Cunxin (pronounced "Lee Schwin-Sing")'s life, so you can learn to pronounce them correctly—as any native Chinese speaker would.

# Li's Family Members

*Cuncia*: Tsoon-say
*Cunfar*: Tsoon-far
*Cunmao*: Tsoon-mow (as in "now")
*Cunsang*: Tsoon-song
*Cunyuan*: Tsoon-yen
*Jing Tring*: Jihng Trihng

## Li's Teachers and Friends at the Beijing Dance Academy

*Chen Shulian*: Chen Shoo-lee-ahn
*Chong Xiongjun*: Chong Shao-joon
*Gao Dakun*: Gow (as in "now") Dah-koon
*Her Junfang*: Her Joon-fang
*Liu Fengtian*: Lee-you Feng-tee-ahn
*Ma Lixie*: Ma Lee-soo
*Song Jingqing*: Song Jihng-chihng
*Wang Lujun*: Wang Loo-joon
*Xiao Shuhua*: Shao Shoo-hwa
*Zhang Ce*: Zang Cher
*Zhang Shu*: Zang Shoo
*Zhang Weiqiang*: Zang Way-chong

## Politicians

*Deng Xiaoping*: Deng Shao-ping
*Hua Guofeng*: Hwa Goo-oh-feng

## Li's Home Province

*Qingdao*: Tsin-dow (as in "now")

# Acknowledgments

To embark on writing my autobiography was an enormous challenge. At times I wondered if I was insane ever to agree to write it in the first place. Then again, I had the privilege of working with two of the most sensitive, caring, and creative editors at Penguin Australia. They skillfully pulled the story out of me and guided me through it in a most fascinating and rewarding process. My publisher, Julie Watts, and my editor, Suzanne Wilson—they are not only two of the best editors one could ever dream of working with, they are also two people with high principles and integrity. Without the sound advice of these two special women and the highly professional team at Penguin, *Mao's Last Dancer* would never have happened. Also to Cathy Larsen, the designer of my book, for her creativity and wonderful design work.

A special thanks to my dear friend Charles Foster, to whom I owe my life and more. He has made an important contribution to this book. The Bandit, Teacher Xiao, Fengtian, and others in China have also helped. And to my beloved parents and all of my brothers back in China who allowed me to tell their stories. They helped me with their recollections of our hard, hard childhood. They endured my endless bombardments—phone call after phone call, letter after letter. To ask them to reflect on those years was like asking them to relive them. They provided me with enormous emotional support in the writing of this book.

And thank you to all my other friends and relatives who helped me with my book and who so enthusiastically supported me.

# PHOTOGRAPH CREDITS

Every effort has been made to trace copyright holders of the photographic material included in this book. The publishers would appreciate hearing from any copyright holders not here acknowledged.

Photographic insert:

"My classmates," "The New Village," "Proudly wearing Mao's army uniform," "My beloved niang," "My first lonely day in Beijing," "The Beijing Dance Academy" (photo by Sarah Darling), "*Hai Luo Sha,*" and "Rehearsing *Hai Luo Sha,*" all courtesy of Li Cunxin.

"First contact with the West" and "On the steps of the Vaganova School," photographs by Ben Stevenson, courtesy of Li Cunxin.

"Defection," photograph courtesy of Charles Foster, Houston.

"*Sleeping Beauty*" photograph by Jim Caldwell, courtesy of the Houston Ballet, "Applying my makeup" (photo by Leticia London, www.leticialondon.com), "*Rite of Spring*" photograph by Jim Caldwell, courtesy of the Houston Ballet.

"With Barbara Bush," courtesy of the George Bush Presidential Library.

"*Esmeralda* pas de deux" courtesy of the Australian Ballet. Photo by Branco Gaica.

"My beloved family" courtesy of the Melbourne *Age*. Photo by Chris Beck.